The Relationship
Doctor's
Prescription
FOR_x

Living
Beyond
Guilt

Dr. David Hawkins

HARVEST HOUSE PU

EUGENE, OREGO

This book contains stories in which the author has changed people's names and some details of their
situations to protect their privacy.

Cover by Koechel Peterson & Associates, Inc., Minneapolis, Minnesota

THE RELATIONSHIP DOCTOR'S PRESCRIPTION
FOR LIVING BEYOND GUILT

Copyright © 2006 by David Hawkins
Published by Harvest House Publishers
Eugene, Oregon 97402
www.harvesthousepublishers.com

Library of Congress Cataloging-in-Publication Data
Hawkins, David, 1951-
  The relationship doctor's prescription for living beyond guilt / David Hawkins.
    p. cm.
  Includes bibliographical references.
  ISBN-13: 978-0-7369-1839-8
  ISBN-10: 0-7369-1839-6
  1. Shame—Religious aspects—Christianity. 2. Guilt—Religious aspects—Christianity. 3. Christian
life. I. Title.
  BT714.H38 2006
  158.2—dc22
                                    2006001338

Printed in the United States of America

06 07 08 09 10 11 12 13 14 / BP-CF / 10 9 8 7 6 5 4 3 2 1

Contents

A Note from the Author

I vividly recall watching cartoons on black and white television when I was a child. As the animated characters strained to make moral decisions, they often had a devil with a pitchfork on one shoulder and an angel, complete with halo, on the other. To do the forbidden deed or not—that was the question.

The caricatures of good and evil are humorous, but the depictions carry more than a little truth. As an adult I still feel at times as if I walk around with the angel and devil in tow, cautioning and tempting me. To do the questionable deed or not—that is still the question.

Issues of false guilt, real guilt, shame, and conviction are not laughing matters. They can help us make good decisions or fill us with needless anxiety and torment. We struggle to do what is right, and we feel pangs of guilt when we make wrong choices—when we simply make a decision we know may displease others.

The Relationship Doctor's Prescription for Living Beyond Guilt will help you recognize the residue of real guilt and show you how to heal from it. You'll learn how to detect false guilt—and how to avoid it. You'll also become more sensitive to spiritual conviction and discover how to overcome painful experiences of shame.

These pages are filled with steps to living a spiritually and emotionally healthier life. Join me on the journey.

1

Listen to Your Pain

For several months, I suffered with a nagging toothache—one of those niggling twinges that wasn't sharp enough to send me to the dentist's office but persistent nonetheless. I tried to ignore it. But the moment I thought it was gone it would show up again, carrying just a bit more pain.

One day while dining out, I bit into a steak and discovered a fragment of broken-off tooth. Apparently, my molar felt it had no recourse but to get my attention in a most egregious way. Desperate now because of the discomfort, I had to make the dreaded phone call. I set up the appointment but told myself I could always call and cancel if the pain subsided. I told myself things were bound to get better. I didn't want a toothache, but I most definitely didn't want to go to the dentist.

I wrestled and wrestled with my ambivalence, all the while whining to my wife, Christie, about the pain and the jagged edge left in the broken tooth.

"Just go in and get it fixed," she said.

"I will—if I have to," I replied. "But I think the pain will probably go away if I give it a little time."

Not surprisingly, it didn't. How could it? The tooth was broken. Finally, I had to face what I'd known all along—this problem was not going away. The tooth would not mysteriously repair itself. The pain would not magically subside.

The pain was trying to tell me something I did not want to hear. I had a problem that required expert care. Yes, it was going to cost me a bundle, but I would be rid of the pain once and for all. I would have to acknowledge that I had a problem and admit that I couldn't fix it on my own. I would need to contact a professional and pay the price before I could be free of the agony I was experiencing.

Embrace the Symptoms

In *The Road Less Traveled,* Scott Peck opens with the now famous words, "Life is difficult." Peck says that once we acknowledge the truth about a situation, we have won half the battle. "Once we truly know that life is difficult—once we truly understand and accept it—then life is no longer difficult."[1]

When I avoided the truth about my bothersome tooth, when I spent time and energy convincing myself that maybe the pain would go away on its own, I created mountains of trouble for myself. Quite literally, I allowed the problem to fester and only added insult to injury. My dentist told me the same thing.

But like so many of us, I didn't want to face the truth about my tooth or about many of my personal problems. And I certainly don't want to admit the truth about that irksome emotion of guilt. I want the guilt I feel—about my failed marriage and the many evenings I spent at work instead of with my family—to disappear, allowing me to live with a free conscience, free from any uncomfortable confrontation with whatever deeper issue the symptom of guilt might be trying to convey. I don't want to have to wrestle with the guilt that comes from regret.

"Life is a series of problems," Peck tells us. "Do we want to moan about them or solve them?" Hmm. Let me think about that one for a moment.

I know that the only real answer to problems is to face them and solve them. But that's not easy. And I can't even begin until I'm willing to confront my symptoms and learn to be thankful for them.

The Art of Facing Things

In *The Book of Awakening*, author Mark Nepo talks about the art of facing things. He shares the wonderful story—one that most of us are at least vaguely familiar with—about salmon that are able to make the remarkable journey back upstream, against all odds. He reveals their secret.

> What the salmon somehow know is how to turn their underside—from center to tail—into the powerful current coming at them, which hits them squarely, and the impact then launches them out and farther up the waterfall; to which their reaction is, again, to turn their underside back into the powerful current that, of course, again hits them squarely; and this successive impact launches them farther out and up the waterfall. Their leaning into what they face bounces them farther and farther along their unlikely journey.
>
> From a distance, it seems magical, as if these mighty fish are flying, conquering their element. In actuality, they are deeply one with their element, vibrantly and thoroughly engaged in a compelling dance of turning-toward-and-being-hit-squarely that moves them through the water and air to the very source of their nature... Mysteriously, it is the physics of this courage that enables them to move through life as they know it directly.[2]

When dealing with the horror of guilt, we must be as faithful to living as the salmon—leaning into the experience, even though we don't like its immediate effects, so that it can teach us and move us forward. The apostle James offers much the same lesson:

"Consider it pure joy, my brothers, whenever you face trials of many kinds, because you know that the testing of your faith develops perseverance. Perseverance must finish its work so that you may be mature and complete, not lacking anything" (James 1:2-4).

Lynn Larkin, in an article titled "Say Goodbye to Guilt," says she sees guilt as a messenger sent to help us be responsible. Her image is of a "pesky little creature flying around my head, annoying me until I do what I need to do to get rid of it." She adds, "This messenger comes to you to let you know you've done something that's not aligned with your values. Your job is to find out what the message is, respond to its message, and allow the messenger to leave."[3]

Identifying the Symptoms

How do we know if we are living with the subtle but debilitating effects of unresolved guilt? Here are a few clues:

- *Excessive defensiveness.* Are you easily offended? Do you have difficulty taking responsibility for your actions?

- *Excessive self-criticism.* Are you overly harsh with yourself? Do you have a lot of inner critical self-talk? Do you have chronic feelings of inferiority and low self-esteem? These are common indicators of unresolved childhood issues.

- *Excessive criticism of others.* Are you critical of others for their faults? Many times people who are hard on themselves are also hard on others.

- *Inability to say no.* Is setting healthy boundaries difficult for you? Do you give excessively to others and have a hard time taking care of yourself? Feelings of inadequacy and shame can make you think you don't deserve good things or to set healthy limits for yourself.

- *Inability to relax and have fun.* Do you push yourself unmercifully? Are you a workaholic? You may have issues you feel badly about but are unwilling to face. Your intensity could be an attempt to mask your pain.

- *A tendency toward depression.* Do you struggle with depression? Do you have a hard time finding joy in life? If you experienced rejection throughout your childhood, your lack of self-worth may now be robbing you of the chance to live a happy life.

These questions will help you determine whether you are living under the shadow of guilt. Certainly, they apply in one form or another to nearly everyone. But if you struggle with these symptoms on a regular basis, you must not ignore them.

You may be wrung out, guilt-ridden, discouraged, and wondering what you have done to deserve the feelings you are dealing with. But let's remember that we all struggle with guilt—real or false, deserved or imagined. Let me emphasize again that the first step is the most important. You must accept your feelings—the full range of your emotions—and listen to what they have to tell you.

Denial

In an odd way, symptoms are our friends—our allies against pain and danger. They appear alongside us and say, "I will help you through this difficult time. I want the best for you. I'm here because I want you to be healed." This is simply the way God has ordered things, and the symptoms of guilt are no different from other symptoms. Try as we might to pretend that we are just fine, that persistent feeling of guilt, whether false or real, won't let go. Like a nagging toothache that won't go away, guilt continues to send its throbbing message: "You must address this issue."

King David tried desperately to deny his problems and his guilt over his adulterous affair with Bathsheba and her husband's murder. We can imagine how this powerful man might have tried drink, food, or sex to rid himself of his inner angst. Maybe he busied himself with ruling his kingdom and focusing his attention on strategic decisions. But, as happens with so many of us, his denial breaks down. The guilt gnaws away at him until he can ignore it no longer.

David says, "When I kept silent, my bones wasted away through my groaning all day long. For day and night your hand was heavy upon me; my strength was sapped as in the heat of the summer" (Psalm 32:3-4).

Who has not been in this place? We wrestle with our illusory attempt to deny problems. We struggle to justify taking money out of the petty cash drawer at work. We rationalize the flirtatious friendship with that office worker, vowing it is innocent and can't possibly lead to a problem. We tell ourselves we are being the best spouses we can be, knowing in our hearts that we are distracted and not giving our marriages all they deserve. Sooner or later, the guilt seeps through our faltering fences of denial.

Even when we are finally ready to listen to our symptoms, we may still be unwilling to seek an accurate diagnosis. In fact, the mixture of confusing voices, along with our own denial, often leads to greater bewilderment. An authoritative diagnosis almost always leads to action—which is precisely why we often run from the diagnosis. Too often we live with our confusion. Why is that?

Denial often provides a respite for us. It is the calm before the storm, the quiet place where we prepare for something we know is headed our way. Some people are able to launch themselves right into the danger zone, but others need time to hide out before facing the enemy. We tell ourselves that if we can have a moment to bolster our strength we will be better prepared to open the envelope and read the diagnosis.

But that respite should not continue indefinitely! Eventually we need to summon our courage, take a deep breath, and move on...

2
Guilt—True or False?

Psychologists have always been fascinated with the topic of guilt. For more than a century we have debated whether guilt is a feeling, an attitude, or an ego state. We have struggled to agree about whether it was something we should work to completely eradicate, foster, or simply ignore. But now almost all mental health practitioners agree that we ignore the symptoms of guilt to our detriment.

Not only have we been unclear about what to do with this thing called guilt, but we have also struggled to agree on a definition. Sigmund Freud and Alfred Adler defined guilt as a fear of losing the love of a significant person or a fear of losing social esteem. Guilt was the consequence of a critical conscience that said we behaved inappropriately.

True Guilt

Jeff, a 55-year-old financial consultant, was quiet and unemotional. His profession allowed him to be alone, scanning worksheets and corporate spending records. He chose a wife who was not prone to exuberance or excessive displays of emotion. He told me he was quite satisfied with their marriage.

Jeff's physician referred him to me because of symptoms of depression, sleeplessness, and decreased appetite. His energy had all but disappeared. Jeff was not interested in acknowledging these symptoms. In fact, he made it clear that he came to me under duress.

I asked Jeff to describe his symptoms in detail, encouraging him to consider why the sleeplessness and loss of appetite had occurred. He declined to open up. He insisted the conversation would be unnecessary because he wouldn't be coming for long. He hoped the antidepressant would alleviate his symptoms. I suggested that the symptoms were windows into what might be bothering him and invited him to embrace them as clues to deeper issues.

Weeks went by with little improvement. Jeff groused that the medication wasn't helping and complained about the cost of seeing me when he could talk to his wife for free. I pointed out that he did not share much personal information with his wife or anyone else. In fact, my working hypothesis was that Jeff was a lonely, detached, and dispirited man who shared his feelings and thoughts with few people. I began to wonder about unresolved guilt—real or false—that he might be carrying around. Did he have real guilt for wrongdoing against his values or false guilt for going against others' values? He seemed isolated from himself and found little joy in his narrow, functional world. Such an existence would make most people morose.

I decided to explore more personal areas of Jeff's life. He was reluctant to allow a stranger into his world, but after some gentle probing and prodding, he loosened up a bit. During one visit, I asked about his physical relationship with his wife, Susan. He assured me he had a very active sexual life—but not with his wife. He sheepishly admitted that he viewed pornography on the Internet and occasionally went to strip clubs.

"How do you feel about what you're doing?" I asked.

"I don't feel good about it. I know my wife would be devastated if she knew, and it goes against my Christian values."

"You're living a double life, Jeff, and somewhere deep inside you're probably feeling a great deal of guilt about it. It's certainly enough to cause anyone to feel discouraged and depressed."

Jeff became noticeably agitated and turned away from me.

"Look. I'm not about to tell Susan, if that's what you're getting at. It would hurt her deeply and probably ruin our marriage. Is that what you expect me to do?"

"Of course not. I want you to feel better. I want you to live a full and vibrant life, free from guilt. Guilt can be devastating to our psyches, not to mention our spiritual lives."

Jeff was upset. Changing the topic, I asked him to share his spiritual values with me. He said he had been a Christian "forever," and he and his wife were active in a community church. He enjoyed the pastor and congregation and felt that his faith was strong. He admitted misgivings about his secret behavior and worried that God would condemn him for his actions.

I told Jeff that God was not the author of condemnation but that He wired us with consciences to help us stay within boundaries so we could live wholesome lives. I pointed out that his guilt was a good sign—he had a conscience and didn't want to hurt anyone or transgress the boundaries God designed.

I pointed out to Jeff that he was experiencing real guilt. Real guilt, as opposed to false guilt, is a natural response to troubling behavior. It is a symptom that points to deeper issues. Jeff reluctantly agreed to explore this further to see how his guilt, and the behaviors leading up to it, might be tied to his depression.

Over the next several months, Jeff and I met on a weekly basis. We explored his fears of talking to his wife of 25 years about his dissatisfaction with their sexual life and his dependence on pornography for satisfaction. We discussed the anger he had toward her for not being sensitive to his needs, and he admitted that he had never talked to her about them. We discussed how he had also gone to strip clubs for sexual arousal and talked about how this was an insult to his wife and to all women.

In time, he took a very bold step and asked his wife to join him in counseling, where he told her about his secret habits. She understandably felt angry, severely disappointed, and betrayed. She vowed to support him in his recovery, but she would need help and time to recover from his blatant actions. Jeff has stopped viewing pornography and going to strip clubs, and he has joined a support group at a local church to meet with men who have similar problems. Jeff has come out of hiding, has sought help for his problems, and is talking with his wife about ways to enhance their intimacy. She recognizes that their relationship had withered over the years and is receptive to improving their communication and intimacy. Jeff's guilt is gone, his depression has lifted, and both he and his wife are feeling hopeful.

Jeff's guilt (true guilt) had a specific origin and was fairly quick to heal. He had to eliminate the behavior causing his guilt and practice new and healthier behaviors. Many problems are not as easy to rectify—many times the guilt is not as easy to trace or to treat. Consider Angela's dilemma.

False Guilt

Forty-year-old Angela came to see if I could do something about her chronic low self-esteem. Married for 15 years with two adolescent children, she was generally unhappy. She had been in counseling several times before, always for problems involving her feelings about herself. She shared her story.

"I feel like a failure at whatever I do. I don't feel like I'm a good enough mother, I fail in nearly every area of my marriage, and I think my boss is disappointed with me. I feel like everything is my fault even though I know it isn't. I worry that I'll ruin my children's lives with my moods even though my husband assures me that they are great kids. I can't seem to shake the feeling that something's wrong with me. I collect guilt, and I don't know what to do about it."

At that point, Angela buried her head in her hands and began to cry.

"I told myself I wasn't going to cry, and now look at me."

"From what you've told me, you seem to feel a lot of false guilt—an exaggerated sense of guilt when you haven't done anything wrong. I'm guessing that guilt has been an issue for you most of your life."

She managed a smile and nodded.

"I guess I've felt inadequate and guilty most of my life. I never felt like I could please my parents and now I can't please myself. I need to stop it, but I haven't been able to figure out how."

"We can find solutions for false guilt. You probably know deep down that you are not really a bad mother. You also probably know that you're not really a failure at everything. In fact, just to test my theory, tell me this: What is one thing that you do that makes you feel proud?"

Angela beamed when she told me about her job as a physical therapy assistant. Every day, patients came to the clinic and asked for her by name. She went on to say that her husband loved her and frequently told her how much he cared for her.

"But it never seems to be enough to stop the guilt—the feeling that I should be better, doing more for the people in my life," she said.

"And that points us to the work we must do," I said. "False guilt is like that. It's a habitual response, not really tied to anything we've done wrong. It's often associated with an old feeling we had as kids, trying to live up to a standard or rules set out for us by someone else, usually our parents. The key is to acknowledge that it really is false guilt, not something we literally are doing wrong now."

Angela seemed relieved.

"For the moment I want you to consider how good you feel knowing that your husband and patients love you. I'll bet your kids think you are pretty special too. We'll work on the rest in time."

Angela seemed to accept what I said. She thanked me for pointing these things out for her. She seemed grateful to know that she could learn to let the burden of false guilt fall from her shoulders. Her countenance was softer and more cheerful as she anticipated freedom from the ever-present weight that guilt, even false guilt, can bring.

Tossing Guilt Back and Forth

False guilt often comes from guilt throwers. Some people are guilt throwers, and some are guilt takers. Oftentimes we are both. If, as one of my clients said, you have mastered "the art of guilt," you may be adept at both throwing guilt onto others and receiving it inappropriately yourself.

- Are you overly sensitive to guilt?
- Do you feel extreme regret for real or imagined misdeeds?
- Do you feel excessively sad for things that happen to others, as if no protective layer exists between you and them?
- Are you easily guilt-induced—that is, manipulated to feel bad for things for which you are not responsible?
- Do you feel obligated to help people when you know that what they are asking is their responsibility?
- Do you feel overly responsible, striving to make life "right" for yourself and your family but always feeling like the job is only half done?
- Do you feel overly conscientious, dwelling on every decision to make sure you don't make a mistake?

- Do you feel as if you don't deserve to be happy or that everyone else's happiness must come before yours?
- Do you feel as if you should be happier and that you should not feel any pain or suffering?

Take a moment to consider if a guilt thrower or master guilt inducer is in your midst. If you answered yes to one or more of these items, you have reason for concern. Master guilt inducers can get you to say yes to something even if you have to violate your personal boundaries. They have a way of telling you how things "ought to be" so that your personal values feel wrong. They reinforce your negative self-perceptions, making you feel worse about yourself.

Most of us have rigid, right-or-wrong thinkers in our family systems. A brother-in-law, mother, or father often wants to tell us that what we are doing is wrong. These people have a better way to raise your kids, a better car you should drive, and a better job you should have. In reality, these people are often struggling with their own guilt or their own inadequate boundaries and are stepping on your boundaries in the process.

Trouble Either Way

You have read two very different accounts of guilt. Jeff's guilt ate at him from the inside out. He tried to cover it up, work it away, and deny it existed. But in the end, the symptoms of depression led to the sleeplessness and fatigue that brought him to his knees. He experienced real guilt. He was guilty of violating the boundaries of his marriage, his faith, and his personal integrity. The price became too high, and he began to develop symptoms that hinted at his inner turmoil. Thank goodness. Those symptoms led Jeff's doctor to recommend that he seek help. As a result, he was able to regain his life, his marriage, and his spiritual wholeness.

Angela struggles with false guilt. With Angela's current mind-set, she cannot possibly experience peace. She must achieve perfection, which of course she can never do. When she fails, which is inevitable, she beats herself up, leading to a wide range of accompanying symptoms.

Angela has not been able to intervene in the vicious circle of self-condemnation, low self-esteem, and subsequent depression. Like Jeff, Angela wants relief and has stayed in counseling to alleviate her false guilt. In the end, her symptoms will be her lifeline. They will draw her to silence the cacophony of unrest in her weary mind.

False or real guilt has plagued Jeff and Angela. It has created symptoms that are unbearable at times. They are learning from their guilt, and you can too.

3

Conviction Helps—
Shame Doesn't

As you learn to embrace your symptoms, pray to discern whether you are experiencing real or false guilt. Are you struggling with habits that go against your core values (real guilt) or against someone else's expectations (false guilt)? In addition, you can pray to know whether the Holy Spirit is lovingly convicting you of real wrongdoing.

Unresolved feelings of guilt, whether real or false, are always debilitating. Robert McGee is clear about this:

> There is no burden that produces pain, fear, and alienation quite like the feeling of guilt. Many of us know it as a constant burden. Some of us respond to it like a whipped puppy, beaten down and ashamed. Some of us avoid it through the numbing effects of denial...Perhaps no emotion is more destructive than guilt. It causes a loss of self-respect. It causes the human spirit to wither, and it eats away at our personal significance. Guilt is a strong motivation, but it plays on our fears of failure and rejection; it can never ultimately

build, encourage, or inspire us in our desire to live for Christ.[1]

McGee goes on to say that we can help ourselves by knowing the difference between guilt and conviction. He notes that guilt has a restricted meaning in the New Testament. It refers only to man's condition prior to his salvation. Only the non-Christian is actually guilty before God. He has transgressed the law of God and must pay the consequences. But Christ has removed this guilt and condemnation from Christians.

Then what about the consequences of sin? The Scriptures are replete with examples and directives about living lives of purity and holiness, and the Holy Spirit is sure to enlighten us in the areas where we fall short (John 16:8). The motivation of the Spirit, however, is not to make us grovel or to lower our self-esteem but rather to lead us out of our slavery to sin so we are free to love and obey Christ even more. This is the essence of conviction.

This important concept is wonderfully liberating. On one hand we have all fallen short of the glory of God and sin continuously (Isaiah 53:6), but we have been made alive together with Christ (Ephesians 2:5). We are a "chosen people, a royal priesthood, a holy nation, a people belonging to God" (1 Peter 2:9).

In my life I have struggled with real guilt and with conviction because of workaholic tendencies that led to being negligent as a father and husband. I failed to live out the values and principles I have adopted as a Christian. I have also struggled with false guilt that has come from fearing the disapproval of others, so I have needed to remind myself that my worth does not come from them but from God.

A Commingling of Feelings

I shot a squirrel yesterday. I had been planning this for weeks as I became angrier and angrier at the feisty rodents' incessant nesting in my attic. At first I vowed to rid my world of them. I would simply set out some rat bait; they would eat it and run off and die. Wrong. They ate it but did not run off and die. In fact, they stuck around and built larger nests in my rafters. Even more determined, I asked around for advice about getting rid of these pests.

"Oh, that's easy," one man said. "Just put fabric softener in your attic, and they'll run away from the smell." Wrong! They use it to make softer nests.

"You need to spray some noxious odor into their nesting area, and they'll leave for sure." Wrong again. The sprays failed to rid the squirrels but stunk up the whole house.

"You need to buy a trap." Nope. I personally watched several squirrels saunter into the trap, take the bait, and walk out the other side.

Finally, I purchased a pellet gun and even did some target practicing. Most often, I shot at them and missed by a mile. They scrambled off, hissing at me from high in their Douglas fir haven. Once in a great while I would hit one but apparently only hard enough to knock the wind out of it. The squirrel would topple over, shake its head to clear the cobwebs, and scuttle into the underbrush.

Then one day I watched as a squirrel skittered out of the attic. Quietly, I left the house, took aim, and squeezed the trigger. Down went the squirrel. Dead.

Victory! Man overcomes nature. I had expected to grab the carcass and raise it high over my head for all to see. Instead, I felt a piercing sickness in my stomach. Tears came to my eyes.

Moments before, I had been determined to eliminate this nasty pest, but now I felt only regret. What had I done? I was surprised by my feelings. Was this shame that I was feeling? Did my act cause me to feel less than human?

Maybe the Holy Spirit was convicting me about killing innocent creatures. But that didn't seem likely. I didn't remember any

Scriptures on shooting squirrels. Maybe I was experiencing false guilt. I was feeling bad for something that I should have felt triumphant about. No, I did not feel like a champion. As best as I can decide—and it is not always easy to figure these things out—I felt real guilt. I had violated my own conscience. I did not believe in killing animals, and try as I might, I had not succeeded in dulling my senses enough to transgress that boundary.

I am still trying to assuage my guilt. I killed for a good reason, I tell myself. Squirrels are pests. But my guilt lingers, suggesting that perhaps killing them simply cannot mesh with my values. In the future, perhaps I will trap them and transport them away from my house so that we both can live in harmony. Discerning the difference between real and false guilt and the convicting work of the Holy Spirit isn't always easy. Pray for the Spirit's wisdom to discern the origin and nature of the guilt you feel. This will lead to the proper diagnosis and remedy—which we will discuss later in this book.

Toxic Shame

We have talked about real and false guilt and the conviction that comes from the Holy Spirit. We need to address yet another common malady—the problem of toxic shame. This phenomenon is closely related to guilt, and yet it is even more debilitating. Guilt is the feeling of having done something wrong; toxic shame is the pervasive feeling of actually *being* wrong and bad.

Many of us have grown up with demanding parents who were ready and willing to have us experience a great deal of guilt—all the time. In fact, when we have critical parents, we always come up short and feel a pervasive sense of guilt. Remember, real guilt indicates that we have actually done something wrong. In the spiritual sense, it is akin to conviction, where the Holy Spirit indicates that we have failed in some way. So where guilt and conviction may indicate I have done something wrong, shame says that I am bad from the inside out.

The most damaging thing about toxic shame is that parents instill it into their children. Kids have no way to fight back against this pervasive sense of badness—a guilt-like feeling that isn't attached to a specific misbehavior. Children pick up this sense of inadequacy when parents make them feel stupid, powerless, and inferior, and then they live with this feeling the rest of their lives.

Toxic shame, delivered at the hands of parents, is very debilitating. People sometimes take a lifetime to overcome it. This kind of abusive shame is to be differentiated from yet a healthier kind of shame. John Bradshaw, author of several books on this issue, including *Creating Love*, explains that healthy shame is an essential component of our humanness. Awareness of our limits is a necessary part of our psychological balance. "To be human is to make mistakes, to need help, and to know that there is something greater than ourselves." As adults we get into trouble, emotionally and spiritually, when we try to act in more than a human way because we continue to shame ourselves by...

- acting as if we are perfect
- trying to control everything and everyone around us
- obsessively seeking power
- being patronizing
- criticizing, blaming, and morally judging others
- acting righteous
- being driven to overachieve
- acting as if we are superior to others[2]

Let's look at how this plays out.

Cindy grew up with alcoholic parents. They were not falling-down, unemployed drunks but rather middle-class "maintenance alcoholics" who went to work every day and drank most evenings. Because of her parents' obsession with drinking, Cindy felt rejected much of the time. She had to care for her younger sister because her parents were either out with friends or watching television. They repeatedly told her to "take care of yourself." Subsequently, Cindy learned that she was of little worth to her parents, aside from what she could do for them. She learned that the only way to win their approval was to be good, which translated into being perfect. She learned to be an overachiever and to find her worth outside of herself through what she could do. She felt a pervasive sense of shame because her parents seemed chronically displeased with her.

Cindy has done nothing to deserve this. In fact, I would consider her a model citizen. But now, as an adult, she feels that she never measures up. She feels bad even when she has done nothing wrong. Her parents have quit drinking and have been more accepting of her actions, but she still feels as if they disapprove of her. This is confusing and hurtful. She struggles to overcome a core feeling of unworthiness. This is the very heart of shame.

Many people struggle with feelings of shame. To them, shame may feel like guilt, but when they stop to sort things out they realize they have never felt truly accepted for who they are. In fact, they have never developed a healthy sense of self—their feelings of worth have always depended on someone else's view of them. Guilt makes people feel that they should have done something differently and is usually tied to an event or situation. But shame is an ever-present feeling that isn't connected to anything in particular. It is almost always linked to childhood issues.

Another difference between shame and guilt is that shame operates on an unconscious level. Repeated rejection during childhood creates an internal process whereby children (and later, adults) reject themselves. The child is rarely able to figure out what is happening, but anger and resentment are always bubbling just beneath the surface. This makes healing all the more difficult later in life.

What distinguishes normal shame from excessive or toxic shame? The answer lies in the consequences of that shame. If, for example, we feel ashamed of ourselves for always arriving 15 minutes late for work and we can alter our behavior accordingly, this is healthy shame. When it does not cause us to doubt ourselves, then it is normal and healthy.

If, on the other hand, the shame impairs our sense of well-being, leads to low self-esteem in our relationships, or causes us to develop a core belief that we are bad people, this is unhealthy.

Unhealthy shame almost always originates in early family relationships. During childhood we learn to honor and respect ourselves and others (or we learn not to). If we are raised in a positive atmosphere, we gain an accurate and realistic appraisal of our strengths and weaknesses and develop a balanced approach toward ourselves and others. But if our families did not model these attitudes and behaviors, they can be very difficult to learn later in life.

Paul mentions this accurate self-appraisal as well as the incredible value we have as Christians in his encouraging words to the Romans:

> Do not conform any longer to the pattern of this world, but be transformed by the renewing of your mind. Then you will be able to test and approve what God's will is—his good, pleasing and perfect will. For by the grace given me I say to every one of you: Do not think of yourself more highly than you ought, but rather think of yourself with sober judgment, in accordance with the measure of faith God has given you (Romans 12:2-3).

He goes on to encourage every believer to exercise the special gifts each has been given. These gifts make every person special and necessary to the family of God.

Acceptance

Anne Lamott, in her amusing book *Traveling Mercies,* offers us a lesson about acceptance. She explains how she warred with herself about forgiving the mother of a friend of her son, Sam.

> It might have astounded her to learn that we were enemies. But I, the self-appointed ethical consultant for the school, can tell you it's true. Somewhere in the back of my mind I knew she was divorced and maybe lonely, but she also had mean eyes. In the first weeks of first grade she looked at me like I was some kind of Rastafarian draft-dodger type and then, over time, as if I were a dazed and confused alien space traveler.

Lamott tells of repeatedly trying to like this woman, only to find everything she did annoying. Lamott cried out to God to help her forgive and accept this woman, but everything the woman did went against Lamott's grain and against her feeble ability to forgive and accept her.

Then, with the kind of epiphany we all desire, she says she got it.

> I got it that I am as mad as a hatter. I saw that I was the one worried that my child wasn't doing well enough in school. That I was the one who thought I was out of shape. And that I was trying to get her to carry all this for me because it hurt too much to carry it myself...I wanted to kiss her on both cheeks, apologize for all the self-contempt I'd been spewing out into the world, all the bad juju I'd been putting on her by thinking she was the one doing harm.[3]

As Lamott reveals her foibles and her ineptness at being a "good Christian," we too can take comfort in our ineptness at forgiving ourselves and others. Lamott begins with where she is. She is vulnerable and humble and very transparent.

The place to begin is right where you are. You will do well to accept that you may have some baggage that you need to unload on this journey. Your parents undoubtedly had some of their own that they needed to deal with, and some of it has probably found its way down to you. So start where you are. Accept what is before you and let's get on with it.

In these first three chapters, we have touched on several symptoms of living with unresolved feelings of guilt. The next section will provide help with diagnosis. Here we will explore more about whether you are struggling with real guilt that needs attention, false guilt that needs to be processed, or unhealthy shame that has been debilitating to you. We will learn about the importance of making an accurate diagnosis and how that can lead to seeking the right remedy.

4

Why Do I Feel Guilty Before I've Done Anything Wrong?

Listening to symptoms of guilt is one thing. Determining where they came from is something much different. Listening to our symptoms is rarely easy, but knowing exactly what these feelings of guilt, shame, and conviction may be trying to tell us is even more difficult.

One of your first tasks, which we prepared for in the first chapter, is to prayerfully consider whether or not the symptoms you are experiencing are the result of real guilt (perhaps you have violated your conscience and values in some way), false guilt (you are trying to fulfill others' expectations for your life), conviction (the Holy Spirit calling your attention to a particular area of your life), or shame (that debilitating feeling exacerbated by some person in your childhood years).

I am convinced that we often flail about needlessly because we are not very skilled at knowing what we are feeling. Worse yet, we are unable to determine what to do about these feelings. To tune into your inner life and determine exactly what you are feeling is no small task. Saying that you are not feeling well is not enough.

Yes, this is a start, but it is about as helpful as telling your physician that you don't feel well. You know the first question he or she is bound to ask:

"Where does it hurt?"

I ask you the same thing.

Why are you reading this book? What are the symptoms from which you want relief?

These symptoms, if you listen to them closely, will lead to a diagnosis and eventually to a remedy. However, getting to that point is no easy matter. In fact, before you are able to receive an accurate diagnosis, you will probably experience one or more false starts.

Some time ago Jerry, a childhood friend, called me to revisit memories and reestablish the strong bond we had once known. I was delighted to hear from him. When I met him for lunch, however, he looked bedraggled. His beard was scruffy, his eyes hollow. No longer the short, fidgety youth I had known 40 years earlier, he now walked with stooped shoulders and spoke with hesitation. He was clearly troubled about something and wanted to see me not just as a friend but also as a professional.

We met at a coffee shop near my house and talked idly for a few minutes. Then he got to the point. "I'm not happy, David," he said. "I have been to a number of different health practitioners, but they can't find anything wrong. They want to give me pills for depression, but I don't think I'm depressed. They want to keep doing more tests, and I'm sick of it. I don't want more tests. I want to feel better."

"What's causing this, Jerry?" I asked.

"How about everything?" he said. "I lost my mother last year, I don't have many friends, and I hate my job. My girlfriend left me two years ago, and I'm lonelier than I've ever been."

"Are you seeing a counselor?"

"I've gone to a couple, but it never feels quite right. It's like I don't connect with them. I did call the pastor of the church I used to attend, and he seems to care what happens to me. He talked to me about loss and grief and guilt, and that made sense. I like him and will probably see him again."

We talked further about spiritual matters.

"I haven't been going to church in recent years," Jerry added, "and feel bad about that. I used to have a strong Christian faith, but now I don't know what I think. I keep feeling like I should go back to church, but I'm not sure where to go. I would love to be a part of a group of caring Christian friends again. A few years ago, I was part of a wonderful Bible study group and was also active in a growing men's ministry. But I let that part of my life slide. Things haven't felt right since."

We talked at length that day. Jerry was clearly depressed—physically, emotionally, and spiritually—though he was in no mood to hear that diagnosis. I could also tell he was feeling conviction from the Holy Spirit about living a life apart from God.

I could not diagnosis Jerry that day, short of affirming that he was lonely, angry, and discouraged—a feeling he has had for some time. He was separated from any sense of community, and his relationship with the Lord was distant. He needed a fresh infusion of love from neighbors, friends, and God. Jerry needed a decisive diagnosis about his condition, and once that was done, he needed to follow through with the recommendations if he wanted to truly feel better.

For now I strongly encouraged Jerry to keep talking to his pastor. He had made a connection that helped him. He had found someone willing to listen to him and share God's love in a tangible and practical way. This was a good start. Professional counseling and a trip to his physician might follow.

Jerry is like many of us—we have plenty of symptoms but stop short of assessing the true source of our pain. As a result, we are unable to make the diagnosis that can lead us to a healthy life.

We have talked about the symptoms of guilt and how unresolved guilt can be manifested. But we must also discuss the sources
of guilt. Only when we identify the source of our guilt can we make
the diagnosis that is critical for positive action to occur. What are
some possible sources of our guilt?

Perfectionism

Probably the greatest source of false guilt is perfectionism—that
inner voice that says you can do more, be more, achieve more. Perfectionism is both a driver for great expectations and a reminder
that you are not achieving enough. When you compare yourself to
this standard of perfection, you can never achieve enough.

As you consider whether or not you are futilely attempting to
attain some impossible goal, go back even further and determine
who set this goal for you. Are you living your own life, or have you
adopted someone else's expectations?

Steve Chandler, author of *17 Lies That Are Holding You Back*,
talks about the effect of living with the lie of personal inadequacy
that comes from perfectionism. "There is a kind of voice in us, that
says it is not safe to live on purpose. It's not safe to express yourself
completely in living your true life. That's too big an adventure for
someone who has done something wrong. That's too big a risk for
the defective person to take, the voice says."[1]

Maybe the goals you are trying to achieve aren't even your own.
Perhaps you have adopted standards that are simply too lofty. You
have set the bar too high and can never reach it. Trying to attain
the unreachable is not virtuous—it's an act of abuse that will only
lead to perpetual guilt. And if you are attempting to live up to
someone else's expectations, you will most probably never find
true satisfaction.

Dr. Kevin Leman offers more insight in his book *Measuring
Up*. "The person who is a defeated perfectionist generally has a
conscience that's way too big. So big, in fact, that it magnifies

shortcomings and failures and won't let its owner forget sins or imaginary sins of years ago, even though they have long since been repented of or paid for."[2] Consider whether perfectionism is an accurate diagnosis for your condition by answering the following questions:

- Do you feel as if you can never measure up, regardless of how well you perform?
- Do you constantly strive to measure up to others' standards?
- Do you set unrealistically high standards for yourself—and possibly others?
- Do you always try to please others?
- Do you have trouble forgiving yourself for past mistakes?
- Do you review your past failures and mistakes?
- Do you blame yourself for others' problems?
- Do you have difficulty accepting God's forgiveness?

Rejection

Many people harbor guilt and shame that have come from chronic rejection. Those who have been raised in troubled, dysfunctional families know all too well the overwhelming remorse that rejection can generate.

Consider the plight of the person raised in a family where parents chose alcohol and escape over active, responsible parenting. Abandonment was rampant—the only attention the children received was negative attention. The parents made the children feel as if they were a burden. They did not honor and adore the children as the beautiful gifts from God that they were. The children felt guilty because they were unable to make their parents happy, but in reality their parents weren't capable of being happy because they were looking at life through the bottom of a bottle.

Unfortunately, a little rejection goes a long way. Early destructive experiences are incredibly difficult to resolve because they seem to make us more vulnerable to rejection and hurt later in life. As an adult, you may have a wonderful marriage and yet still feel especially sensitive to rejection and feelings of guilt and shame. You may know that your marriage is solid and strong and yet fear your mate may walk away from your relationship. Your "self" may feel very fragile.

Dr. Charles Whitfield, in his pioneering work *Boundaries and Relationships,* offers this insight:

> One of the most frequent problematic feelings is low self-esteem and shame. After all, why would anyone abandon me unless I am somehow inadequate or bad? So when another leaves me, without a healthy self with healthy boundaries, I may feel not only inordinate amounts of shame, but I may also be vulnerable to taking on and absorbing any other person's projected shame that is not mine. With few and sometimes no healthy role models, and with repeated invalidation and rejection of my feelings of fear, shame and other emotional pain, I may end up with the core issue of difficulty handling feelings in general.[3]

If early rejection and abandonment were central issues in your life, you may have significant healing work to do. Consider the following questions.

1. Were you raised in a significantly dysfunctional family with physical, emotional, or sexual abuse?
2. Were you raised around addictions, such as alcoholism or drug abuse?

3. Were you raised in a family that did not allow the open expression of certain feelings?

4. Were you raised in a family where each individual was less important that the whole family?

5. Were you raised in a family that overtly or more subtly encouraged you to keep quiet?

6. Were you raised in a family that did not encourage your uniqueness as a person?

If you answered yes to any of these questions, this may help explain your sensitivity to rejection and point to a need to heal old wounds.

Emotional Abuse

What if you had a relatively normal childhood and entered adult life filled with awe, wonder, and a future of limitless possibilities, only to find yourself in a marriage fraught with manipulation, twisted words, mind games, sarcasm, distance, and demands—in short, emotional abuse? You had no way of preparing for this. You did not see it coming. Now, after years of this kind of treatment, you feel as if you've been shot out of a cannon and left to bleed to death.

A bit dramatic, you say? Hardly. If you have lived in a world of emotional abuse, you know the feeling. Words can hardly describe the feeling of being loved one minute and despised the next.

This kind of abuse occurs every day in countless marriages. Some women are adept at speaking with confusion, and some men can manipulate words to make women think up is down and down is up. Again, if you have been there you know what I am talking about. In these homes, false guilt is an all-consuming experience. You can do nothing right, and nothing you do can possibly make your spouse behave differently.

Patricia Evans, author of the book *The Verbally Abusive Relationship,* helps us understand what is taking place:

Verbal abuse is damaging to the spirit. It takes the joy and vitality out of life. It distorts reality because the abuser's response does not correlate with the partner's communication. The partner usually believes the abuser is being honest and straightforward with her and has the same reasons for what he says. Since the partner does not understand her mate's motives, she "lives in hope."[4]

If you are living with emotional abuse, you need support. Don't try to face this alone.

Childhood Abuse

Childhood emotional, physical, or sexual abuse is incredibly debilitating. Tragically, this unholy destructive combination often occurs together. Children raised with emotional abuse often have experienced physical abuse as well. We also know that childhood sexual abuse occurs far more frequently than is ever reported or admitted.

If you have been raised in a world where people repeatedly invaded protected arenas of your life, if you have felt unprotected and violated, if your naive world has been shattered, you may have overwhelming feelings of guilt and shame. You may feel that someone treated you this way because something is wrong with you.

Having worked with many victims of abuse, I have found that they can't quite shake the feelings that they are bad. Even though they know they have done nothing to deserve their treatment, the feelings of being bad linger. This is often because the abuse is larger than any single event. It is larger than a one-time incident of being hit or molested. It is about not being protected in the first place, and then not having a safe place to talk about it and recover from it. The whole world becomes a dangerous place.

John Bradshaw, in his book *Creating Love,* helps us understand the child's world. Children, he says...

are deeply trusting. Children bond with their parents and have a survival need to believe that their caretakers are okay. Children are egocentric, which means they personalize everything. If a survival figure yells at them, it is about them, not about their survival figure's headache. The words that children hear impact them greatly. The words they hear continue to play in their heads and become voices that are self-nurturing or voices that blame, criticize, compare, and express contempt. Children internalize their parents at their worst. When parents are screaming, raging, hitting or sexually violating a child, the child's security is most threatened.[5]

Dr. Matthew McKay offers us further insights into this problem.

Early sex or physical abuse frequently contributes to a feeling of being "damaged goods," unworthy of any love or happiness in life. When tragedy strikes, pervasive shame and guilt make it seem like well deserved punishment rather than simple bad luck.[6]

If you have experienced the horror of emotional, physical, or sexual violence, you may have feelings of fear, guilt, and shame that you cannot shake. You may have voices in your head that you cannot silence. If you have experienced early abuse, your very self may be shattered. Recovery from this serious diagnosis often requires professional help.

Codependency

Codependents have a particularly rough time with guilt. After all, their boundaries are diffused. They take on others' feelings. When others are feeling good, codependents feel good as well. When others are feeling bad, codependents feel as if they are doing something wrong. Their sense of self is fragile and vulnerable.

Denise is a 60-year-old woman who came to see me because she was unhappy with her marriage. An attractive woman with long, brown hair, she looked years younger than her age. She wore a T-shirt from a recent trip to a coastal town near my office. She had a broad smile and seemed generally happy except when she talked about her marriage. She shared an almost unbelievable story.

"I know my husband is cheating on me. He's had a girlfriend for the last ten years. I even caught them together at a local restaurant. I walked right up and confronted them about their relationship. Most of the time he says it's just a friendship and won't give it up. But he has told me before that he cares for her."

"How do you feel about this?" I asked.

"I hate it. It makes me feel sick and bad about myself. I'm furious at him, but I can't make him stop it."

"What have you done to insist that he stop seeing her?"

She looked dazed for a moment, perhaps puzzled by my question. I persisted, gently.

"Have you told him he must stop it or you will separate from him?" I asked. "Have you told him that what he is doing is intolerable?"

"Well, I tell him. But I don't want to leave him. I don't believe in divorce."

"I'm not talking about divorce, Denise. I'm talking about telling him that your marriage is something sacred and that you cannot tolerate him seeing another woman."

Denise simply stared at me as if she had been beaten down one too many times.

"I don't know if I can really set that limit with him. I'm afraid he might leave me for her. He's said that if I keep pushing he might do just that."

"Yes," I said. "That's a risk you may have to take if you want to insist on purity in your marriage."

Denise has yet to set any firm boundaries with her husband, and at this time he is still seeing the other woman. She is so dependent on her husband for the few good feelings she has about herself that she dares not risk making him angry. He has found a way, through fear and intimidation, to keep her helpless, dependent, and guilt-ridden.

Although we may want to scream at Denise, "Why are you tolerating such indignity in your marriage?" her inaction is not unusual. Many others like her tolerate similar but perhaps less profound abuse. Harriet Goldhor Lerner, in her book *The Dance of Anger*, says, "If we are guilty, depressed or self-doubting, we stay in place. We do not take action except against our own selves and we are unlikely to be agents of personal and social change."

Fighting against this inertia is very difficult, she says. "If we are serious about change we can learn to anticipate and manage the anxiety and guilt evoked in response to the countermoves or 'change back' reactions of others. More difficult still is acknowledging that part of our inner selves fears and resists change."[7]

Perhaps you are enduring an intolerable situation out of fear. You must know how this erodes your self-esteem and makes you feel angry, resentful, and guilty. Let someone help you work on feelings of codependency and set healthy boundaries in your life.

5

Truth and Consequences

In the previous chapter we explored some of the sources of our nagging feelings of guilt, shame, and conviction. These sources— perfectionism, rejection, abuse, and codependency—are often difficult to confront head-on until we recognize they have often grown out of experiences that were beyond our control. But as we listen to our symptoms, we can proactively and courageously face the underlying sources of our pain, making ourselves available to God's healing touch.

Now, let's move forward, taking a candid look at where we're coming from so we can find our way to a better place.

Unforgiveness

Unforgiveness has long been described as a reservoir of bad blood. It is a cesspool of negative emotions that poisons our feelings about ourselves. We know that we are harboring resentment toward that old friend for rejecting us. Our gut knows that we still resent that parent for preferring a sibling over us. Our heart knows that we can't quite get beyond being passed over for promotion at work.

We all have disappointments that will turn sour unless we resolve them. We are not meant to be containers for grudges, resentments, and feelings of revenge. Although these feelings are perfectly natural, they can harm us in the long run by creating bitterness and dissatisfaction. They can turn a good mood into a bad one. But getting rid of them is easier said than done.

Forgiveness is hard. I get angry when I hear Christians pontificate about forgiving as if we could throw a switch and end all the bad feelings toward someone who has wronged us. This is perhaps one of the clearest demarcations between God and man—God can and has forgiven us. We, on the other hand, wrestle with our ambivalence between wanting to forgive—and knowing this to be God's will for us—and wanting to squeeze every bit of juice out of resenting someone that we can.

I have taken a long time to forgive a former colleague for deeply hurting my feelings. He rejected me, refusing to return my calls or offers to meet for lunch, at a time when I needed his support. I still don't know his reasons for pushing me away, but I have tried to be understanding about it. I'm trying not to take his rejection personally, but I have carried the residue of unforgiveness. The path has not been easy, and any counsel that presumes it should be is not helpful. Forgiveness takes intention, understanding, seeing things from his point of view, and prayer. Even then it is still not a simple matter, but I have made definite gains.

Are you wrestling with unforgiveness? Don't worry. I'm not going to preach or tell you what you already know—that it hurts you more than it hurts them. But I will encourage you to practice letting it go. You will only be a container for guilt and other bad feelings if you rehearse your wound.

Gail Sheehy, noted authority on the passages of life, tells a story in her book *New Passages* of sitting with friends and making the following observation: "It's almost as if you have to forgive the things that happened in the first half of life—the people who failed you and the ways you failed yourself—in order to go into the second half."[1] This does seem to be our work if we want to be happy.

Unresolved Anger and Resentment

Perhaps a combination of the above situations fits your life. Perhaps you have tolerated far too much abuse and violence, and they have left you resentful and angry. On the other hand, there may be no major violation in your life, just a series of small but damaging circumstances that you have put up with for too long.

I have learned that resentment is a robber of mental health. Resentment—anger that we keep sending out, over and over again—takes a toll on us. It eats away at our peace and tranquility. The Scriptures address this issue: "My dear brother, take note of this: Everyone should be quick to listen, slow to speak and slow to become angry, for man's anger does not bring about the righteous life God desires" (James 1:19-20).

James admonishes us to first be *quick to listen.* I don't know about you, but my anger and resentment are immediate blocks to me hearing anything. When angry, I want to blurt out my opinion. I want to tell others that they are wrong. I want to win, win, win. I do not want to be humble and suspend judgment long enough to really hear what others are saying. Moreover, I don't want to hear anything about my role in the problem.

James goes on to say we should be *slow to speak.* Again, the reasons for this are obvious. When we speak in a measured, considered way we are less likely to be offensive, rigid, and demeaning. When slow to speak, we are more likely to let others have their say. This is a great relationship builder.

Finally, James says we are to be *slow to anger.* Why? Because anger is often destructive and breeds resentment and guilt. Who has not suffered the effects of an out-of-control temper? Who has not longed to be able to take back harsh and biting words? I certainly have. Anger almost always causes problems, and problems often lead to appropriate guilt. Dr. Mark Goulston, in his book *The 6 Secrets of a Lasting Relationship,* agrees:

> Nothing cramps enjoyment like the accumulation of anger, resentment and other negative feelings between partners. Obviously, overt hostility will utterly destroy enjoyment, unless you happen to enjoy fighting. It's hard to find pleasure in being with someone who has done something to enrage you—or is seething with animosity toward you.[2]

For years, we psychologists were telling people, "Vent your hostility. It will be good for you." It was incredibly bad counsel. We now know that the only thing venting does is create even more hostility—and make you sick and guilty to boot. So, if anger and resentment are problems in your life, let someone help you explore the healing power of forgiveness.

Regrets and Mistakes

I have told many clients struggling with a lifetime of mistakes that we cannot make it to 35 without feeling some regret and remorse about life—provided we have consciences, of course.

By the time we hit 35, most of us have been married, had children, and made some serious mistakes. Who among us has reached midlife without having made some significant error? How many of us have navigated through those early decades without having encountered some personally destructive experience? Not many. In fact, most of us have multiple blunders to our credit long before we reach the midway point in our lives.

I have been working with a 43-year-old woman who is closing in on her second divorce. Even though her husband was verbally and physically abusive, she blames herself. She belittles herself and feels guilty for subjecting her three children to a divorce, a disparaging and critical stepfather, and now another divorce.

Sitting discouraged in my office, Sandy shared her heart.

"I should have known better. I didn't do a very good job picking out my first husband. Then I made matters worse for the kids by marrying Gene. He has been overly critical with the kids and me, and I feel horrible about that. I look back and see that I picked Gene because he was a stable provider and gave us a nice standard of living. That was a terrible mistake. I overlooked his flaws, and my kids had to suffer as a result."

Sandy's work will be difficult. She must find a way to deal with her mistakes and regrets. She must grieve the losses that cannot quickly be soothed. Those losses are real; her regrets are honest. She will have to take a fearless inventory of her mistakes and transform them into new insights and opportunities.

Failure

Failure is impossible to avoid and very difficult to manage. Failure is often so pronounced in our hearts and minds that denial rarely works. Merely saying the word produces a knot in the pit of my stomach, reminding me of times in my life when I simply let myself and others down. We cannot dodge these feelings. Perhaps you can readily identify events in your life that were nothing less than outright failures—and the guilt still stings.

I sat today with a man who was dejected about life. Only 39, Jake looks nearly twice his age. His hair was uncombed, his face unshaven. His clothes hung limply on his body. He was a walking advertisement for misery and failure.

Jake had been beaten down by a series of mishaps, missteps, mistakes. "I am so depressed about the way things have been going in my life. Here I am, thirty-nine years old, and I don't own a house. I still rent. How embarrassing is that? I've been involved in three businesses, and every one has failed. We can't really pay our bills, and I see no way out of the financial mess we're in. My wife and I both work, but with four kids and all the debt from my failed business ventures, we're still not making ends meet. I've started college many times and dropped out each time. I still don't know exactly what I want to be when I grow up. Do you hear that? A thirty-nine-year-old man admitting that he still hasn't grown up."

Working with Jake is a challenge. He always has a reason to explain why positive change cannot take place. Every time I come up with a suggestion, he says he's tried it before. In his opinion, nothing can possibly work because he's a failure.

Jake didn't believe he had made a *few* blunders. He wasn't just tripping over a handful of mistakes. In his view, *he* is a mistake. *He* is a failure. The stumbling blocks in his life have become an insurmountable mountain. I haven't given up hope with Jake. But he will have to look once again at each disappointment and failure and slowly transform all of them into meaningful and thereby important aspects of his life. If your diagnosis is similar to Jake's, your work will be difficult. But you *can* do it.

Sin

We finish this section on sources of guilt with a discussion of possibly the most disturbing topic—sin. Frankly, even thinking about sin makes me squeamish. I want to hide from the topic, perhaps because I know the truth: "For all have sinned and fall short of the glory of God" (Romans 3:23). And that is the defining issue—missing the mark of what God wants for us. It is also the source of much guilt and conviction because we have fallen short of God's standards.

The Holy Spirit brings conviction to our lives, and He always does it for our good. Let me make sure you caught that last part— conviction is *always* for our good. The admonitions of the Holy Spirit are like the words of a loving father encouraging his child to wear a helmet when bike riding. This counsel does not come from a critical parent intent on catching his son doing wrong. The counsel comes from a loving father who wants his son to play safely, to protect himself, to live a life filled with wonder and joy.

But perhaps you have grown up under the influence of a great deal of legalism, where your spiritual standing is tied to your behavior instead of your heart and faith. If you were raised in a demanding, legalistic family or church, you may see God as a tough and exacting taskmaster. Perhaps you have been listening to the sermons that bellow out how you are a doomed sinner and can only expect judgment for all your sins. Thankfully, the Scriptures encourage us and offer us grace. Listen to John's words:

> And now, dear children, continue in him, so that when he appears we may be confident and unashamed before him at his coming. If you know that he is righteous, you know that everyone who does what is right has been born of him (1 John 2:28-29).

John wrote these words under the inspiration of a loving and grace-filled Father God. We are encouraged to do what is right, to avoid "missing the mark" so that we can have fellowship with Him.

But we do miss the mark. We do fail. We do fall into sin, try as we might to avoid it. How does this square up with doing what is right? Fortunately, that is what the cross is all about. The apostle Paul clarifies the issue: "Therefore, there is now no condemnation for those who are in Christ Jesus, because through Christ Jesus the law of the Spirit of life set me free from the law of sin and death" (Romans 8:1-2).

I love the parable of the lost son, recorded by Luke. In Luke 15 we read of the younger son who asked his father for his share of the estate, only to "set off for a distant country" where he "squandered his wealth in wild living." If anyone has reason to feel guilt and shame, this young boy does. He has every reason to suffer for his actions. Should he ever return, he must tuck his tail between his legs and pay dearly.

Time passes, and we read that "he came to his senses." The boy decides that life is better back home even if he has to work as one of the hired hands. As he nears his home, he rehearses his words—he will tell his father that he has sinned against heaven and against his father.

Did you notice that this youth can see that his sinful ways are not only against his father but also against God the Father? Selfishness, pride, and lascivious living not only are damaging to us but also violate our loving God's standards.

So our young man walks the lonely path toward home, ready to eat with the pigs and sleep with the servants. But something miraculous happens—for the young boy and for us as well.

"But while he was till a long way off, his father saw him and was filled with compassion for him; he ran out to his son, threw his arms around him and kissed him." Amid protests from the boy's older brother, the father threw a party and welcomed his son back home.

This story poignantly illustrates an important truth: We *will* miss the mark. This is part of our nature. But we can experience true joy when we turn back and seek God's loving and forgiving heart.

Responsibility

The potential sources of guilt are practically endless. Making an accurate diagnosis about the possibility of guilt and moving forward with your life will include taking full responsibility for what is happening with you. Listen to your symptoms and then take responsibility to find help and make an accurate diagnosis that will lead to the appropriate remedy.

As long as we hide behind blatant denial, we cannot make a decisive diagnosis.

This may seem obvious, but many people like to blame their emotional and spiritual plight on others. Jerry, my friend from childhood, was like that. I noticed a subtle anger beneath his discouragement. He wanted someone to come and rescue him from his problems and instantly make things better. Of course this was not going to happen. Denise, who was living with an unfaithful husband, was eaten up by resentment. Poor boundaries resulted in her repeated victimization, which led to further resentment and guilt.

How do we take responsibility for our lives and emotions? Drs. Jordan and Margaret Paul, in their book *Do I Have to Give Up Me to Be Loved By You?* get us started:

> To have both freedom and intimacy we must understand what it is to be personally responsible to oneself and to others…Each human being has the freedom of choice over his or her own actions; all of us are accountable for our choices and their consequences. No other person can be responsible for the feelings that result from our choices, whether they are happy or sad.[3]

Each of us is responsible for responding to the actions that lead to our guilt. We are also charged with dealing directly with the guilt throwers in our lives. We must respond to those who would make us feel bad for not visiting more often, not getting better grades in college, or not living up to some other standard they have established for us. We must learn to act constructively with our guilt—and doing so is the topic of our next chapter.

As we move through this book, you are learning how to embrace your symptoms, seeing them as friendly messengers rather than bearers of bad tidings. You have also learned more about the importance of understanding the sources of your guilt.

Now we will move to the best part: the remedies for those pesky—I mean, helpful—feelings of guilt. In the next section, we will examine some tools for dealing with real and false guilt, feelings of shame, and feelings of conviction sent by the Holy Spirit.

6

I Was Wrong—Now What?

The year was 1969—a time of turmoil, triumph, and transition. Gas was 35 cents a gallon. Tuition at Harvard University was $2000 a year. Woodstock drew half a million people. Richard Nixon was president, the country was deeply divided over the Vietnam War, and I graduated from high school—barely, and then I came down with asthma.

I remember the onset as if it were yesterday. I woke up one morning, unable to breathe, frightened and confused. My parents assumed I had a cold and had me hovering over a boiling pan of water most of the day, my chest slathered with Vick's VapoRub. But my breathlessness did not abate. I wheezed and coughed and gasped for air. By evening I was admitted to the ER. Diagnosis: adult onset asthma. My lungs were losing their elasticity and wouldn't function effectively, especially under exertion. A tough call for a teenager who liked to swim, snowshoe, mountain bike, hike, and ski.

Making the diagnosis was the easiest part of the journey I was about to embark on. The remedy was a far more arduous ordeal.

My parents and I soon discovered everyone had a cure for

asthma. We began with a chiropractor. My parents heard that chiro-practors could cure anything. Several hundred dollars later, armed with salves and natural remedies and having undergone numerous adjustments, I was wheezing as much as before.

With a persistent inclination toward natural remedies, my par-ents took me to a naturopath. This was an even greater disaster. I remember lying on an examining table, wheezing and groaning and being forced to ingest a bizarre tincture of ground butterfly wings, cornstarch, and beetle juice! While naturopaths reportedly do wonders for some folks, I would have had more confidence if Peter Pan had sprinkled fairy dust in my face and implored me to "Just believe, David."

Then came the allergist. I was losing hope. Again many people told my parents they had tried allergists and achieved positive results. The doctor at the allergy clinic poked me until I felt like a pincushion. Apparently, I was allergic to every common substance on the earth. The allergist prescribed shots twice weekly, and I was told to stay away from furry animals (I had a dog and cat), pollen, and dust. Did he think I was going to live in a contaminant-free bubble? To be fair, I think the shots actually helped.

My next experience came several months later after I moved to Seattle to study at the University of Washington. I met a hippie-doctor from the University of Washington who ran a free medical clinic. Dr. Hughes took a liking to me and an interest in my medical plight. I recall going to his home several times a week for percussive treatments—whacks on the back to loosen phlegm—and taking suppositories and steroids. This combination, along with good old-fashioned TLC, was actually quite helpful to me. I slowly began some of the physical activities I had enjoyed earlier.

With hospital visits on the decline and life taking on a greater sense of normalcy, nearly a year later I was transferred from the free clinic to an internal medicine specialist. Dr. Farnsworth reevaluated me for the umpteenth time and determined that I did, indeed, have asthma and could live a rather normal life with a bronchodilator, a prescription to clear my lungs, and preventive medicine. With these medications, my hospital visits ended and life was normal.

No more hospitals, no more butterfly-wing tea, and no more human pincushion. I'm done with percussive treatments, though I sort of miss the free clinic attention that included midnight tea with Dr. Hughes. Although I would certainly prefer not to have asthma, the worst is over. I must be cautious and keep a bronchodilator with me, but I've run the Portland Marathon four times. We paid attention to my symptoms, made a clear diagnosis, and found the appropriate remedy.

Your Personal Search for a Remedy

As you have worked through this book, you may have gained some idea about what ails you—whether it is real guilt from mistakes you've made, false guilt from an overbearing family member, or shame from the residue of perfectionist or abusive parents. Your symptoms will lead to diagnosis, which leads to remedy. I hope your search for a remedy for your feelings of guilt will be shorter than mine for asthma! If you are fortunate, you suffer from no ailments at all. Instead, the soft but penetrating voice of the Holy Spirit (conviction) is wooing you to a holy life.

As you consider your particular issue, your unique problems will lead to your unique remedy. As with most medical dilemmas, each guilt experience requires its own treatment plan. One size does not fit all. That is why I cannot offer a simple platitude and expect it to solve your problems. Instead, you need access to an array of treatment options.

Before we begin seeking and applying a remedy, let me remind you that you need to be clear about what you are feeling and why. This clarity sets the stage for the proper remedy. If you are struggling with false guilt from an overzealous guilt thrower, repenting of sin will not make you feel better. If you are struggling with the sticky residue of shame subsequent to sexual abuse as a child, your course of action will be very different than it might be if you are dealing with real guilt. Consider your particular problem and its unique remedy.

To prepare for our discussion on remedies, take a moment to answer the following questions:

- Have I committed serious mistakes for which I feel natural regret and real guilt? If so, how have I handled those feelings?

- Has a master guilt thrower made me feel guilty for not measuring up in some way? Who was that person, and how have I handled those feelings of false guilt?

- Has someone violated me in some significant way or neglected me earlier in my life, and has this led to feelings of shame and inadequacy? How have I handled those feelings of toxic shame?

- Have I felt the conviction of the Holy Spirit for something in my life? How have I responded to those feelings?

You can see that your answers to these questions will offer powerful clues to the remedy. They will provide you with directions to the appropriate cure. Let's now look at the remedies for various forms of guilt and shame.

Remedies for Real Guilt

Stan is a 36-year-old electrician, tall and muscular with hands heavily calloused from hard labor. He spoke softly and without humor or animation. Stan told me he had been plagued by depression for years and had finally sought counseling for his symptoms. After several sessions we determined that real guilt was a primary culprit in his problems.

"I feel badly for how I've lived my life. I was a practicing alcoholic for a decade and destroyed my marriage and my relationship with my two sons. I was gone a lot and came home drunk most nights. My wife finally told me to get out. That was enough to make me get sober, but by then it was too late for us."

"What have you done with your life since that time?" I asked.

"I'm active in AA, and it's saved my life. I go to church but nothing else except work."

"How about your kids? Do you still see them?"

"I see them every now and then. They're good kids. My ex-wife did a good job with them. They're 14 and 16 and more attached to their stepfather than to me. I failed them. I think they don't really want to see me."

Stan looked blankly at me. Sadness and guilt were written all over his face.

"You have plenty of regrets."

"I sure do. I should be making an effort to see my kids more often and reestablish a relationship, but I don't. I just feel so bad for what I did. I know I can't make it up to them, so I've stopped trying."

"I'm not sure I agree that you can't make it up to them, Stan. I know about regrets. I have my share of them myself. But I don't know that it's ever too late to be a good father to your kids. You can't erase what's happened, but you can admit your mistakes and be a part of their lives. Don't you think they'd like to see you more?"

"I'm not sure. I don't know how to go about making a change. I feel stuck."

"I know this may sound overly simple," I said, "but the way to begin is just to begin. It's not likely you will ever get over your guilt until you make amends for what you've done and begin to act differently."

Stan nodded.

"I guess that's why I'm here. I just need a little moral support to help me face up to my mistakes and get on with things."

Stan did make amends to his sons, though this did not translate into an earth-shattering, sky-opening experience. His healing happened the way most people's do—by putting one foot in front of the other. Mountains are reduced to boulders one stone at a time.

Let's consider a few things that helped Stan deal with his real guilt and might be helpful to you.

- *Stan took responsibility for failing his kids.* He had reached the point where he could look in the mirror and talk about his specific failures. Stan joined the ranks of the rest of us who have failed and lived to tell about it. None of us are perfect. But we can take responsibility for our failures.

- *Stan apologized for his mistakes.* He had to say those oh-so-difficult words: "I'm sorry." He had to show his sons that he felt bad for failing them and demonstrate that he was willing to change.

- *Stan needed support in taking his first step.* He made significant progress simply by reaching out to me for moral support. Many people, especially men, have a hard time asking for backup. They feel as if they have to do things on their own, so they falter when taking that initial step.

- *Stan had to take things slowly.* He had to change his behavior. He could not naively hope that every simple step would meet with success. In the long run, he would achieve significant change.

- *Stan had to follow through with the behavior change.* Making the first move was one thing; following through with the next 20 steps was something entirely different. We don't usually eradicate guilt with one act of contrition. Only a series of heart-changing behaviors will show others that we mean business.

- *Stan had to forgive himself for his failures.* He had to

accept forgiveness from himself and from God. He had to recognize that he couldn't change his past, but he could determine how he wanted to live his future. Each positive step could help him overcome past failures.

Stan worked through his real guilt, using these tools and steps. Change was not instantaneous, but several weeks of counseling left him feeling better. Stan suffered from real guilt that required real behavior change.

The apostle Peter also had to work through real guilt by grieving his failures. You may recall that Peter had a brief conversation with Jesus during one of their last meals together.

"Simon, Simon," Jesus said, "Satan has asked to sift you as wheat. But I have prayed for you, Simon, that your faith may not fail. And when you have turned back, strengthen your brothers."

Simon, in typical fashion, starts talking: "Lord, I am ready to go with you to prison and to death."

Jesus answered, "I tell you Peter, before the rooster crows today, you will deny three times that you know me" (Luke 22:31-33).

This must have seemed ludicrous to Peter. Although he had made mistakes before, to hear that he would deny Jesus surely felt like a slap in the face. For all of his foibles, Peter was a loyal follower. For years, he had sat at Jesus' feet, drunk wine with Him in celebration, and learned from the Master. To find out that he would deny even knowing Jesus could not have made sense. But it happened.

After the temple guards led Jesus away and took Him to the house of the high priest for questioning, Peter followed "at a distance." Here is our first clue that Peter is losing his courage. Next, a servant girl recognizes him and says, "This man was with him."

In that split second, Peter has to decide if he will take the high road and face ridicule or the low road and face his conscience.

"Woman," he says haltingly, "I don't know him."

A few minutes later another person says, "You are one of them."

Here was a chance to redeem himself by acknowledging his loyalty to Jesus. Instead, he failed again.

"Man, I am not."

An hour later another confronts him. "Certainly this fellow was with him, for he is a Galilean."

"Peter replied, 'Man, I don't know what you're talking about.' Just as he was speaking, the rooster crowed. The Lord turned and looked straight at Peter. Then Peter remembered the word the Lord had spoken to him: 'Before the rooster crows today you will disown me three times.' And he went outside and wept bitterly" (Luke 22:54-62).

He wept bitterly. Here was a broken man, wracked with guilt. He had disappointed the Lord and fallen far short of his standards. Here was guilt in full force, the gut-wrenching agony that comes from violating one's conscience.

Fortunately, the story does not end here. Peter must have grieved his failure, sought forgiveness, and moved on with his life and his mission. In fulfillment of Jesus' prophetic name for Peter—the Rock—the book of Acts shows Peter taking a leadership role in the formation and functioning of the church. On the day of Pentecost Peter addresses thousands and informs them about the working of the Holy Spirit. His name is woven throughout the chronicles of the early church as a leader. Although Peter had disappointed his Lord, Jesus established a transforming relationship with him and entrusted him with leading the church into the future.

Defeating the Invisible Giant

Real guilt is one thing; false guilt is an entirely different matter. When we violate our conscience, we change our lives and move ahead. But when we struggle against perceived violations, falling short of others' expectations or being the target of someone else's arrows, moving forward can be much more difficult.

Remedies for False Guilt

The most important strategy for dealing with false guilt is to *differentiate it from real guilt*. This is essential for obvious reasons. Consider the following story.

Danielle was a pleasant, soft-spoken 42-year-old who had been married for more than 20 years before her husband, Steve, sought the affections of another woman. Shortly thereafter, he asked for a divorce even though Danielle said she was willing to forgive him and remain in the marriage. Their two daughters were now away at college, and she had been alone for two years.

Danielle appeared sad and understandably angry as she talked about her husband leaving her. She shared that she had hoped this would be a time when they would be making retirement plans. Anger was not her chief complaint, however. She talked more about the doubts she had about herself and her shaky future. She talked about her fears that she was unworthy of a new relationship.

"I have some friends who try to coax me into going out. But I just don't feel like I measure up. Steve used to always tell me to dress differently, walk differently, even talk differently. I was never enough for him, and he finally proved it by finding a new model."

"So what does his finding another woman mean to you?" I asked.

"It tells me something must be wrong with me for him to give up 20 years of marriage and walk out on everything we built together."

"I'm curious about something," I said. "Did you ever think his expectations might be inappropriate? That the problem might be his?"

"I thought about that. But it's pretty tough to have someone look you in the face and tell you he doesn't want you anymore. I feel like it all comes back to me."

"Your hurt has to be very deep. Losing your marriage was a terrible thing. But can you try to separate your loss from feelings of false guilt—those feelings that seem like real guilt but aren't realistic?"

"Sometimes I can, sometimes I can't," she said. "I keep coming back to the fact that he left me. He didn't want me. I wasn't enough for him. He essentially told me I could never be enough for him. I had too many imperfections. He was critical of how I dressed, the way I kept our home, and that I didn't earn the kind of money he wanted me to earn."

"Separating what you might have done wrong in the marriage from what he might have you *believe* you have done will be the heart of your work."

Danielle's journey may be similar to yours. You may be like Don

Quixote, jousting at imaginary windmills, never able to defeat the real enemy—others' inappropriate expectations of you. Your task is to strengthen the volume of these voices so you can silence them. Yes, let me say that again: You must turn up the volume of these voices, give them names, and then change the channel by contrasting their message with what you know to be the truth.

Let me offer an example from my life.

I have struggled with workaholism for most of my life. Both of my parents were ambitious and modeled hard work. Although they carved out time for play and we had a very happy family, I learned that a nose-to-the-grindstone approach was the way to get ahead in life.

You may be wondering what is wrong with this message. Nothing. And everything. I have struggled to find a balance between work and play, just as my parents did. I have struggled to measure up. Even though I worked some 16-hour days and brought work home on the weekends, I still had the nagging feeling that I did not work as hard as my colleagues or others who were successful in business.

So what is my task? I must make sure that I turn down the volume on the voice that tells me...

- You are only as good as your work.
- You must always do the absolute best you can.
- You must do more.
- You must always give the company 110 percent.
- Your value lies in what you can produce.
- You must always put work first and play second.
- You should always take your work seriously.

My task is to contrast these messages with the truth and what the Scriptures say. So I reflect on how I might best respond to these statements.

- You are much more than what you do for a living or how much work you can produce.

- The quality of your work could sometimes be better, but what you are doing is sufficient.

- You don't always need to do more.

- You don't owe the company 110 percent.

- Your value does not lie in what you produce. It lies in your character and God's image in you.

- Interspersing play with work is all right. In fact, work can and should be playful at times.

Let me offer another example from my personal life. My parents and four siblings have told me in many ways that I *ought* to visit them more often. My siblings seem to be more devoted to visiting our parents than I am, and I have struggled with this. Turning up the volume on their message, I hear…

- When will we see you again?

- Mom and Dad are not getting any younger. This is a time when you should be visiting more often.

- You owe it to visit more often.

I listen carefully to my values—my truth—and I hear…

- You love your parents deeply, but you have a life apart from them. You visit them as often as is consistent with your chosen lifestyle.

- Rather than visiting out of obligation and false guilt, you can visit because you miss them and want to spend time with them.

- Rather than bowing to the pressure of family, you should act from your values, doing what feels right to you.

- You will convey to your parents how much you care for

them in ways that are consistent with your values and character.

Can you see the process that must take place to eliminate the burden of false guilt? Can you see the dialogue that must occur to reduce the power of the guilt throwers and strengthen your character?

A word of caution is in order, however: When you stand up to the contrary voices, they may not back down easily or quickly. If you are working against a pattern of control that has occurred for some time, identifying and verbalizing your values and desires may be an arduous task. Stating your opinion and living out your unique life takes practice. Do not expect everyone to champion your individuality.

Dr. Kevin Leman, in his book *Measuring Up,* offers additional suggestions for dealing with false guilt:

- *Don't pile one infraction on top of another.* When you have a failure, deal with one issue at a time. Be careful about running down a list of all the ways you have failed to live up to your standards or someone else's.

- *Don't take the blame for other people's problems.* Guilt-ridden perfectionists often have a lot of "guilt buttons" and are ready targets for others' anger. When your mate comes home upset after a difficult meeting at work, be careful about assuming that his mood is your fault. When your boss is temperamental, use caution instead of assuming you must have done something to create his negativity.

- *Don't believe you deserve to suffer.* People with guilt problems often assume that things go wrong because they deserve to have bad things happen to them. This is faulty thinking.

- *Don't believe you should be judged by what others think*

of you. This is the heart of false guilt—trying to live up to others' standards. Don't try to live up to their expectations. Live up to your own expectations. And be sure they are yours!

- *Don't be afraid to take steps to change.* Living the way you've always lived is easy, but change is the only way to a healthier life. Take a deep breath, say a prayer for courage and strength, and start setting boundaries that define your standards instead of automatically bowing to what others expect of you.[1]

Remedies for Toxic Shame

We have already talked about the diagnosis of shame in one's life—how it often surfaces in response to severe abandonment or emotional, physical, or sexual abuse. Perhaps you are troubled by a feeling of being flawed to the core. You cannot shake your feeling of badness regardless of how many times you read Scriptures that tell of your worth as a child of God. You feel as if you've done something wrong and need to rectify the situation.

False guilt says others think I am doing something wrong; shame says something is wrong with me as a person. If you feel this way, shame may be the culprit.

John Bradshaw called toxic shame "the shame that binds you." He says toxic shame...

> is experienced as the all-pervasive sense that I am flawed and defective as a human being. Toxic shame is no longer an emotion that signals our limits, it is a state of being, a core identity. Toxic shame gives you a sense of worthlessness, a sense of failing and falling short as a human being. Toxic shame is a rupture of the self with the self.[2]

A reading of Bradshaw's recommendation for healing toxic

shame is clearly reminiscent of God's remedy for healing toxic shame in the book of Genesis: *coming out of hiding*. You will recall that Adam and Eve, after breaking God's law, felt ashamed and went into hiding. Their healing required them to come out of hiding, and the same is true for you and me:

> To heal our toxic shame we must come out of hiding. As long as our shame is hidden, there is nothing we can do about it. In order to change our toxic shame we must embrace it...Embracing our shame involves pain. Pain is what we try to avoid...In the case of shame, the more we avoid it, the worse it gets. We cannot change our "internalized" shame until we "externalize" it.[3]

Bradshaw recommends the following steps:

- Develop relationships in which you can share your honest feelings.
- Choose relationships with people who view you with respect, not shame.
- Work on reducing your shame by validating your feelings. Writing and talking about past shaming experiences will help you "legitimize" your feelings.
- Learn to recognize parts of yourself you have buried away. Bringing them to the surface ("externalizing" them) will help you embrace them and work with them.
- Make decisions to unconditionally accept yourself as a whole. Learn to say, "I love myself for..." Become more assertive by voicing your needs and wants.
- Allow unconscious memories to surface. Work on accepting them and moving forward toward healing.
- Learn exercises to bring out the voices in your head. Replace them with nurturing, positive voices.

- Learn to recognize who shames you, and practice assertive techniques when around them.

- Learn how to handle mistakes and have the courage to be imperfect.

- Create an inner place of silence through prayer and meditation where you feel centered and grounded.

We are indebted to Bradshaw for his thorough work on the issue of shame. His list of remedies has been very useful to me in my struggle with workaholism and my subsequent divorce. I have found journaling to be a particularly effective tool in helping me to get the "other voices" outside of my head and get clear about what I believe the Lord may be saying to me.

I was raised in a strong Christian home that espoused working hard and being committed and married to one person for life. These are solid Christian values, and yet they don't make me a good or bad Christian. The Scriptures tells us that God looks on the heart, not on externals. I have had to remind myself that my failure to lead a balanced life with my work, the subsequent losses that came from that, and my failure and inability to keep a marriage intact do not bring condemnation from God even though other people may look down at me. My task is to be clear about what the Lord expects and how He calls me to live my life, and to live accordingly.

During my daily quiet time, I describe what I feel, think, and want in my journal. I sometimes write out a prayer to God—a prayer of thanksgiving for all He's doing in my life, a prayer of petition for help, a prayer for those in my life who also need His divine grace. I pray for clarity—what He is saying to me and what my values are as opposed to what others might expect of me. These are powerful tools in the fight against feelings of toxic shame.

The 12-step program says we are only as sick as our secrets. In *The Message*, Eugene Peterson offers this counsel from Galatians 6:2: "Stoop down and reach out to those who are oppressed. Share their burdens, and so complete Christ's law. If you think you are too good for that, you are badly deceived." Peterson paraphrases Paul's words in Romans 15:1-2 this way: "Those of us who are strong and able in the faith need to step in and lend a hand to those who falter, and not just do what is most convenient for us. Strength is for service, not status. Each one of us needs to look after the good of the people around us, asking ourselves, 'How can I help?'"

The remedy for toxic shame rests on establishing a connection with others and sharing your inner pain. It hinges on allowing the church to do what it is supposed to do—sharing the healing love God has for us and that He gives us for each other.

Will you let it do that for you? Will you find a small group where you can be transparent and share your inner pain? If so, you will be on your way to ridding yourself of toxic shame.

8

A Light at the End of the Tunnel

Light is a curious thing. At times we desperately want it—as is the case during dark periods of our lives when we are searching for answers. A little light can be appreciatively bright during these dark times.

At other times light can be piercingly unwelcome, as is the case with conviction. At those times we may not want the light at all. Light often brings conviction.

Feelings of conviction are different from feelings of real guilt, false guilt, and toxic shame. Although the feelings can overlap, conviction is the *loving* work of the Holy Spirit that creates change from the inside out. Conviction brings the light of clarity and truth to the darkness of dishonesty and sin.

Don Miller, in his book *Blue Like Jazz,* provides a great illustration of conviction. He tells how he spent years being critical of boring, dishonest, hypocritical churches:

> Here are the things I didn't like about the churches
> I went to. First: I felt like they were trying to sell me
> Jesus. I was a salesman for a while, and we were taught

that you are supposed to point out all the benefits of a product when you are selling it. That is how I felt about some of the preachers I heard speak…And yet another thing about the churches I went to: They seemed to be parrots for the Republican Party.

He explains how he had been struggling to find a church that offered him the things he needed: spirituality, artistry, community, and authenticity. (This, by the way, may not be what you need from a church.) After years of struggling with painful feelings, he shares the following insights:

> I read through the book of Ephesians four times one night in Eugene Peterson's *The Message,* and it seemed to me that Paul did not want Christians to fight with one another. He seemed to care a great deal about this, so, in my mind, I had to tell my heart to love the people at the churches I used to go to, the people who were different from me. This was entirely freeing because when I told my heart to do this, my heart did it, and now I think fondly of those wacko Republican fundamentalists, and I know they love me, too, and I know we will eat together, we will break bread together in heaven, and we will love each other so purely it will hurt because we are a family in Christ.[1]

Let me draw your attention to several important things here.

First, Miller immersed himself in the Scriptures. Hebrews 4:12 says, "For the word of God is living and active. Sharper than any double-edged sword, it penetrates even to dividing soul and spirit, joints and marrow; it judges the thoughts and attitudes of the heart." Miller allowed himself to be pierced by the Word of God, by the work of the Holy Spirit. The result was conviction. The remedy was to change his attitude, with God's assistance.

Then, after reading Scripture, Miller feels conviction. He says that he was influenced by Paul's desire that Christians get along. Miller feels conviction and obeys. Please note that hearing the voice of the Spirit is one thing, but obeying is quite another. Here we see Miller listen and then follow. He tells his heart that it is time for a change. He begins to see those who are different from him as simply different, not bad.

Finally, we see the result of obedience to the Spirit's conviction—freedom. He begins to live his life in accordance with what the Spirit of God desires for him. He no longer fights with other Christians and their beliefs but now sees them in an entirely new and freeing light.

Like Miller, I sometimes tend to dislike those who are different from me. As I stroll around my neighborhood I notice the tall, barrel-chested deputy starting his car, readying himself for work. Mike is stiff but friendly in a "don't come too close, neighbor" kind of way. He totes power as surely as he carries his gun and badge. My first, second, and third reactions are to criticize him in my mind, mocking his stance, being uncomfortable with his all-consuming authority. But then I hear the quiet voice of the Holy Spirit saying, "Easy does it, David. Let go of your fears. For Mike to be different is okay. He's just doing his job, and besides, he needs love and friendship as much as you. Be kind. Look beneath the surface. Love him just as I love you."

How is the Spirit of God convicting you? Can you hear the loving voice of God calling you in some new direction? Perhaps He is asking you to let go of some resentment. Perhaps He is inviting you to draw closer to Him.

As you listen to the loving voice of God, as you read the Word of God, you will feel the importance of changing according to His plan for your life.

Abiding in Christ

Although all of the remedies we have considered can be valuable, the ultimate remedy for living beyond guilt and shame is abiding in the protective love of Christ. All of our earthly maladies find respite in Him.

The psalmist David had his share of problems, not the least of which was guilt. He says, "O Lord, hear my voice. Let your ears be attentive to my cry for mercy. If you, O LORD, kept a record of sins, O LORD, who would stand? But with you there is forgiveness" (Psalm 130:2-3).

Although David offers me hope, he also gives me pause. If this "man after God's own heart" couldn't stand before God unafraid, where does that put me? The truth is, it puts me at God's mercy, which is precisely what I cry for daily. I must remind myself that God's grace is just that—grace, unmerited favor. Nothing I will do can ever cause Him to love me more or less.

The apostle Paul says, "For he has rescued us from the dominion of darkness and brought us into the kingdom of the Son he loves, in whom we have redemption, the forgiveness of sins" (Colossians 1:13).

Tucked away in my Bible on an old stained and wrinkled piece of paper is a quotation by the great Quaker spiritual leader Hannah Whitall Smith:

> We all know that growing is not a thing of effort, but is the result of an inward life principle of growth. All the stretching and pulling in the world could not make a dead oak grow; but a live oak grows without stretching…The essential thing is to get within you the growing life… "Hid with Christ in God," the wonderful divine life of an indwelling Holy Ghost…Abide in the vine. Let the life from Him flow through your spiritual veins.[2]

I presume that Smith draws her inspiration from Jesus' words in John 15 concerning the vine and the branches. This metaphor of the Christian life reveals a vital principle:

> I am the vine; you are the branches. If a man remains in me and I in him, he will bear much fruit; apart from me you can do nothing. If anyone does not remain in me, he is like a branch that is thrown away and withers; such branches are picked up, thrown into the fire and burned. If you remain in me and my words remain in you, ask whatever you wish, and it will be given you (John 15:5-7).

Without the infilling love and power of Christ, we will falter and fail. All the remedies we know are insipid without God's power. I strongly encourage you to bathe your issues in prayer, asking God to equip you with the power to identify your problems and put the necessary remedies into action.

Checkup

By now you have identified symptoms, begun to formulate a diagnosis, and started piecing together a remedy that will lead to physical, emotional, and spiritual health. This is a good time to pause and reflect on your situation.

Have you listened carefully to your symptoms, embracing them as guides to an accurate diagnosis and subsequent remedy? Have you considered which areas of your life need change? Have you immersed yourself in the Word of God for wisdom that is applicable to your situation? This is no time for avoidance or denial. This is no time to pretend that everything will be fine tomorrow. Denial most often leads to disaster.

Richard Mayhue offers this account of the sinking of the Titanic in *A Christian's Survival Guide:*

> At 2:20 A.M. on April 15, 1912, the impossible happened. The unsinkable ship sank. The most celebrated

cruise ship in all of history nose-dived to the Atlantic bottom. It had sailed four days earlier from North Hampton, England on its maiden voyage en route to New York; no expense had been spared to make it the most gala cruise ever. All went according to schedule until Sunday night when the Titanic sailed into an ice field.

She had received four warnings of impending danger that day from ships who were in the midst of the ice, but she chose to ignore all four—several did not even reach the bridge of the captain. At 11:00 P.M. that Sunday night the wireless operator, John Phillips, received a direct warning call from the California which was ten miles away in the midst of some very large ice.

Phillips was tired, having sent messages all day to America. So that night he cavalierly tapped back, "Shut up, shut up, I'm busy." Forty minutes later the beloved ship of the White Star Line collided with an ice behemoth. Within hours she rested in her watery grave along with 1,500 passengers and crew, certainly one of the world's great human disasters.[3]

The moral of this tragic story is obvious. How many of us are too busy to read the danger signs? How many of us want to resist the warning signals of real and false guilt, shame, and conviction? Each can teach us valuable lessons if we are willing to pay attention.

Although we are wise to heed the symptoms and use wisdom to seek an accurate diagnosis and remedy, how much better to apply an ounce of prevention!

Let's now consider some things you can do to live free from guilt and shame.

9

Living in the Light

On May 18, 1980, Mount Saint Helens erupted, and my new home was swept away by the massive mudflows of the Toutle River. Twenty-four years later to the day, I left for work in the morning only to return to another flooded home that evening. The 1980 eruption and subsequent loss was an "act of God," but the flooding of my home in 2004 was an act of stupidity on my part.

I had decided to do a load of laundry. Nothing wrong with that idea, except I failed to follow the conventional wisdom that says you should never leave home with your washing machine, dishwasher, or dryer running. Not that anything is likely to happen—but it could. And, in my case, it did.

The water sensor on the washing machine failed.

After I left for work, the washer ran. And ran. And ran. I arrived home to find water four inches deep in my living room and pouring into my lower-level garage.

To say that my heart sank would be an understatement. I have come to appreciate my home as a sacred refuge from the storms of life. It has been my retreat and sanctuary, far from the ravages of the

Toutle River, overlooking the tranquil waters of Case Inlet on Puget Sound. I felt sick as I observed the destruction. More importantly, I was disgusted with my own cavalier attitude that things like this could happen to other people but not touch me. I had failed to take an ounce of prevention—the simple act of turning the machine off as I left my house—and now I would have to pay the price.

I spent the next 12 months sorting through water-soaked memorabilia, clothes, sporting goods, and other personal items. I hadn't anticipated the emotional damage. I cried countless tears over my immeasurable losses and had trouble pulling myself together.

I filled a huge dumpster with personal effects that had been ruined. I had to leave for several weeks as repairmen worked to restore my home. The pound of cure was an extremely expensive lesson.

The lesson about prevention applies to our spiritual and emotional lives just as it applies to flooded houses. Let's consider how it might be relevant for you.

Reaping and Sowing

The Scriptures are clear about a vital principle—we reap what we sow. If we plant corn, we will reap corn. If we plant potatoes, we will reap potatoes. There is no way around it. We cannot get corn from carrot seeds or oranges from plum trees. The irreversible fact of nature is also an irrefutable principle from the heart of God.

> Do not be deceived: God cannot be mocked. A man reaps what he sows. The one who sows to please his sinful nature, from that nature will reap destruction; the one who sows to please the Spirit, from the Spirit will reap eternal life. Let us not become weary in doing good, for at the proper time we will reap a harvest if we do not give up (Galatians 6:7-9).

I have shared with you a destructive tendency in my life—

working too much. As I struggle to find balance, I recognize the inviolable laws of nature that affect my body. I am forced to pay closer attention because I tire more quickly, which reduces my working hours. As much as I would like to change things, I can no longer work the long hours I worked as a younger man. I can no longer function on four or five hours of sleep regardless of how badly I would like to do so. I need more rest and relaxation to function effectively and to do the work God has called me to do.

Knowing what I need and following those guidelines are sometimes two different things. When I push the envelope and try to function on five hours of sleep, I become irritable. I suffer, as do those around me. When I work too hard or too long, my counseling becomes less effective. Working harder and longer, with inadequate rest and recreation, wreaks havoc in my life.

In recent years I have viewed my actions from several different angles. In some respects, my behavior has addictive qualities. I have gone to a number of men's groups to try to deal with this malady. I have seen other men struggle with the same issues and watched as they changed their lives for the better. This has helped me work toward a healthier balance in my own life.

I have also considered my behavior from a spiritual perspective. I recall Dr. James Dobson explaining how he too struggled with maintaining balance. He shared a Scripture about reaping and sowing that I have found helpful: "I am the true vine, and my Father is the gardener. He cuts off every branch in me that bears no fruit, while every branch that does bear fruit he prunes so that it will be even more fruitful" (John 15:1-2).

Notice that the Father, as Master Gardener, knows when to cut back the branches so that the remaining fruit will be even better. I recently watched apple growers in eastern Washington go through their orchards and cut off branches loaded with perfectly good apples. I was perplexed by their actions until the orchardist explained that the remaining apples would be even larger and sweeter. Healthy apples were pruned to give others the opportunity to grow.

Our lives are much the same. We can accomplish many things, but the things we do with balance and the Lord's blessing will be the sweetest of all. Although I might sometimes try to dodge these scriptural truths, making all sorts of rationalizations and excuses, I cannot avoid them. When I ignore the fact that my life must have balance, I pay a price. What I reap in my life I also sow.

As I have reflected on this issue, I have found remnants of inadequacy and shame in the recesses of my mind. For many years, I chalked up my behavior to a simple desire to get ahead. But that rationalization didn't explain things completely. If that were true, for example, why didn't I slow down at the first sign of fatigue? Why didn't I stop when I earned enough income to satisfy our family needs?

A closer inspection revealed feelings of inadequacy and a desire to prove my worth by accomplishing more than the next guy. Feelings of shame were intertwined with those feelings of inadequacy. In my desire to obtain my father's approval, perhaps owing in part to my place as the middle child, I had unwittingly determined that the best way to do this was to "be more." I have had to work hard to stop planting destructive seeds that lead only to disappointment and do nothing to heal my inner wounds.

Planting Seeds of Prevention

In my search for inner healing I began to consider what would happen if I planted new seeds in my life. What if I sowed a harvest of prevention? As surprising as this may sound, I had not really considered that I needed to plant healthier seeds. I naively thought that things would simply work out positively for me regardless of the kinds of seeds I sowed. Did I really have to tend my emotional and spiritual life? Did I need to nurture my well-being? In short—yes. And so do you.

Let's examine how life looks when we practice healthy, life-sustaining principles—the seeds of prevention—an approach most doctors recommend, regardless of their specialties. Our goal, after all, is not simply to eliminate our symptoms. We want to live emotionally and spiritually healthy lives.

Let's consider the life of one who cares for soul and spirit in such a way that guilt—both false and real—is foreign. Let's reflect on what life might be like if we took such care of ourselves that shame became a stranger. And what if we lived a life so filled with the spirit of God that conviction was not a haunting feeling but rather a gentle, welcome touch?

Preventing Real Guilt

This one is simple—and the hardest thing you will ever do. To live without guilt we must play by the rules whether we want to or not. The rules of the government, the rules of the school, the rules of the family, and yes, the rules of God.

Perhaps the prophet Micah said it best: "He has showed you, O man, what is good. And what does the LORD require of you? To act justly and to love mercy and to walk humbly with your God" (Micah 6:8). Here is a recipe as good as any for a healthy life. But it comes at a cost. We must live by the requirements. This is not easy for self-centered folks like me who have a habit of living willfully.

Requirements, by definition, demand we must play by the rules. If we do not do what is required, we will experience consequences.

I was recently preparing to take a trip to the Caribbean island of St. Kitts to teach a seminar. I carefully packed my bags, making sure to include my suntan lotion, my medicines and vitamins, my tropical shirts, a few polo shirts, my computer, and other ancillary belongings. I was ready to go and I was proud of my thoroughness. I had made a list and checked it twice!

But just before leaving my house it suddenly occurred to me

that I might need my passport. I scrambled to consider whether this Caribbean island was a foreign country. I decided to be safe rather than sorry and searched frantically for the document. When I couldn't find it, I made a few phone calls. Yes, I would definitely need my passport—no exceptions. Not for doctors or authors. Not even for an Important Visiting Professor. To enjoy this trip to St. Kitts, I had to play by the rules. Fortunately, after sweating a few bullets, I found it and went on my way with a huge sigh of relief and a promise to keep the passport in a highly visible place when I returned.

Let's consider what the prophet Micah meant when he talked about requirements and reflect on how they relate to the issue of guilt-free living.

To Act Justly

Justice implies receiving what our actions deserve. Justice promotes a sense of rightness. By leaving my house while the washing machine was running, I deserved to be flooded. We all take precautions in some areas and push the envelope in others. Justice, however, will eventually be done. Your life will operate according to this principle.

Micah encourages us to act justly toward others and ourselves. He suggests that we use this value in our everyday lives and actively seek ways to treat others with justice. Be fair-minded. Even in times when your emotions run wild and you want to hand someone what they apparently deserve, you might take a moment and consider if dispensing justice is your job. Moreover, a bit of reflection may reveal that other people do not deserve what we originally had in store for them.

To Love Mercy

Ironically, I can be merciless with others while expecting mercy in return. The equation is completely out of balance. I pretend I can feel fine about being impatient with you, but I will instantly become irritated if you are impatient or irritable with me. Yes, this is a flagrant double standard. My only excuse is that I'm human.

Micah shows me I am lacking in this area. I am to love and embrace mercy. I am to practice handing out mercy whenever and wherever I can. I am not permitted to mete out my own brand of justice to those who offend me. I cannot ignore this injunction. Freedom from guilt, in my opinion, comes in part from loving mercy. Somewhere in my spirit, I know that when I am impatient, irritable, and merciless with others, I am displeasing God. Regardless of how hard I try to ignore the truth, my gut always seems to keep score.

Recently I heard the story of a man who came to an intersection, stopped, and suddenly heard a car honking behind him. Incensed, the man jumped out of his vehicle, went to the car behind him, reached in through the window, and grabbed the driver by the neck, threatening him with bodily harm if he didn't lay off the horn. Later, still shaking with anger, he shared his explosion with his wife, who told him she had recently placed a sticker on his bumper that read, "Honk if you love Jesus."

This man had acted impulsively, not knowing the full story. This is certainly the way many of us conduct ourselves. We act angrily because we do not understand the situation. We conveniently ignore the mercy we received when we deserved harsh treatment. We want justice for others, mercy for ourselves. This path inevitably leads to improper actions and a large dose of guilt.

To Walk Humbly with God

This is a tall order. In a world that is so fast-paced, slowing ourselves to a measured walk is difficult. But not only are we instructed to walk slowly, we are told to walk with humility. The Scriptures constantly remind us that we are not to think of ourselves more highly than we ought (Romans 12:3). This includes not valuing our opinions over other people's. It also means checking our opinions against God's. God knows what is best for us, and we would do well to seek His wisdom in our daily lives.

Jesus said that the greatest in the kingdom of God are those who are as humble as children. He said that if anyone wants to be first, he must be the servant of all. The apostle Paul, who wrote almost half of the books in the New Testament, said that Jesus is our model of humility, noting that He "did not count equality with God a thing to be grasped, but…humbled himself and became obedient to death" (Philippians 2:6-8).

Humility means willingly placing yourself in a servile position with others. Paul tells us to "serve one another in love" (Galatians 5:13). This has been called voluntary submission—particularly apropos in marriage. Humility is part of the art of listening to another, forgetting yourself for a moment and actually focusing on what another person is saying to you. Humility is also the art of listening to God, forgetting the busyness of your own life and tuning in to what God is saying through His Word.

The simple truth is that the antidote to real guilt is to live a humble and moral life, guided by your God. If you live according to the Scriptures and the laws of the land, your conscience will be clean.

Chuck is a delightful, older man who lives near me. When I pass by his home on the way to mine, he always has a mischievous twinkle in his eye, a ready smile, and a joke. With well-worn laugh lines around his eyes, a silver Lincolnesque beard, and the ruddy complexion of a man who has spent too much time in the sun, Chuck has lived a good life. This does not mean that he is free from sinful activities, but he uses the Scriptures as his compass to find his bearings when the path becomes obscured.

Every time I walk by Chuck's house we chat about life. He wants to talk more now that he has struggled with cancer. Often he offers some tidbit that I mull the rest of the day, such as remembering we are only on this earth a short time and should make the most of it. Our most recent conversation about the Christian life was no exception, carrying with it the ring of an elder's wisdom. We were talking about making tough decisions in our lives.

"David," he said, "you just need to do what's right. It really is that simple. The Bible says that God has placed right and wrong in our hearts, and we are really without excuse. If you do what's right—if you really try to do what's right—you're going to be fine. If you treat others with respect, follow the law, and honor God above all, you'll be all right. If you follow your personal code of conduct, your moral compass—assuming it lines up with God's values—you'll be fine."

"I don't know if it's that easy, Chuck," I said a bit defensively. "You make it sound like there's nothing to it."

"Whoa. You didn't hear me say it was easy. It's just that as I've gotten older I've gotten tired of the consequences of doing things my own way. God is very clear about this. When we do what's right, we are blessed. I want to be blessed, so I'm going to try to do what is right."

Chuck paused for a moment. When I didn't respond, he continued.

"I'm just saying that I like the blessings that come from following God and doing what's right. I like not getting speeding tickets," he said, clearly aware of my driving history. "I like seeing my wife smile when I surprise her. I like the big grin I get from Ted next door when I mow his lawn when he is gone for the weekend. I like not fretting about getting caught for fudging on my income tax. It's a pretty neat life."

Chuck has it right. He is done casting seeds to the wind and is willing to carefully do the sowing that will bring freedom from guilt. He reminds me of the truth about living with integrity, explaining that the word *integrity* comes from the root word *integer*, meaning *whole*. When we live with integrity, we live true to our moral fiber. We do not live disingenuous lives, filled with falsehood. We practice living true to our calling and, subsequently, experience very little guilt. How are you doing at being true to your calling? Are you living with integrity?

I gave Chuck a bear hug the last time we talked. Just because he deserved one and because I care about him. I trust him because he speaks the truth. And I pray that his cancer doesn't return. I need more voices like his in my life. I think about what he says to me and try to apply it to my life.

10
Staying out of
the Shadows

Try as we might, avoiding the shadows of guilt can sometimes be a most difficult venture. We need keen awareness to guard against unwanted feelings of guilt.

Preventing False Guilt

Even if you are abiding by the speed limit, being honest on your income tax, and even mowing your neighbor's lawn without being asked, you may still feel guilt—false guilt. As we have discussed in this book, some people will always be uncomfortable in their own shoes and intent on projecting that discomfort onto others. To prevent false guilt, you will need to solidify your boundaries so that what guilt throwers feel and believe has nothing to do with you.

This clear sense of self is not easy to come by. Let me offer a few points that will help you avoid feelings of false guilt.

- *Recognize your own values and beliefs.* Develop a clear understanding of who you are, what makes you tick, and how you want to conduct your life.

- *Understand that your life is different from everyone else's life and that they may be critical of your choices.* You cannot please everyone. If you try, you will create tension and unrest within yourself and cater to the weaknesses of the guilt throwers.

- *Identify those who will try to throw false guilt at you.* We must be able to recognize those who are intent on making us feel guilty. Knowing where the darts are going to come from can help us avoid them.

- *Maintain firm boundaries.* Letting others know that even if they disapprove of you or your choices, you are not going to feel guilty or change for them.

- *Understand that failure to develop firm boundaries will create resentment and eventually erode your relationship with the guilt throwers.* Healthy relationships are built on differences. We must not try to change others and must confront those who try to change us.

Preventing Shame

Avoiding shame is a tough prospect. The seeds of shame are often buried deep within the psyche, and preventing it requires real soul-searching and deep personal exploration. The good news is that once the culprit has been excavated and identified, you can become an expert in ending cycles that have caused so many problems in your past. You will know how to bring truth to bear upon shame and how to eradicate it.

Sandy was a 45-year-old woman who had struggled with shame-related issues. Fortunately, she had participated in personal therapy and healing workshops and now carried herself with a strength and resolve to avoid the feelings that had previously paralyzed her.

Sandy was the middle of three children and had constantly battled the middle-child syndrome. Her older sister worked as the superintendent of a small school district, and her younger sister was a prominent attorney. Sandy had chosen the life of an artist and homemaker. She loved to surround herself with her crafts and children, and that was enough for her—except after family gatherings, when she felt ashamed for not achieving more in her life. She often wondered if she should have set higher goals. But she eventually realized that her happiness did not lie in achieving more.

Sandy has learned to prevent shame from accumulating in her life—not that she hasn't found it sneaking up on her at times. But now she is more aware of those old, familiar feelings and the reasons for them. She reminds herself of the truths of Scripture and about the importance of being satisfied with her real identity:

- We all have different gifts (Romans 12:6).
- She is a child of God (John 1:12).
- She has been delivered from Satan's grasp into the kingdom of Christ (Colossians 1:13).
- Christ dwells within her (Colossians 1:27).
- She has been declared righteous by God (2 Corinthians 5:21).
- She is a new creation (2 Corinthians 5:17).
- She is accepted by God (Colossians 1:21-22).

When she is struggling with old, shameful messages, she meditates on this Scripture:

> "For I know the plans I have for you," declares the LORD, "plans to prosper you and not to harm you, plans to give you hope and a future. Then you will call upon me and come and pray to me, and I will listen to you" (Jeremiah 29:11-12).

Sensitivity to Conviction

Guilt and shame are feelings that come from within. They are provoked by either our own actions or other people's intentions. But the feeling of conviction is much different. Conviction is the product of the Holy Spirit. It is a grace-filled nudging—not punitive finger-pointing.

The disciples were saddened at the prospect of Jesus leaving them after His time among them. They knew they would be losing a dear friend and revered leader. But He told them He would be leaving for their sakes. He promised that He would send a Counselor for them—the Holy Spirit. The apostle John tells us about this experience and the future role of the Spirit.

> Now I am going to him who sent me, yet none of you asks me, "Where are you going?" Because I have said these things to you, you are filled with grief. But I tell you the truth: It is for your good that I am going away. Unless I go away, the Counselor will not come to you; but if I go, I will send him to you. When he comes, he will convict the world of guilt in regard to sin and righteousness and judgment: in regard to sin, because men do not believe in me; in regard to righteousness, because I am going to the Father, where you can see me no longer; and in regard to judgment, because the prince of this world now stands condemned (John 16:5-11).

Here we learn that the Holy Spirit will convict the world of sin and righteousness and judgment. The Holy Spirit makes us holy, as God is holy. He does this by convicting us of our sin and by bringing us humbly to the foot of the cross. The Spirit convinces us of God's love and forgiveness and of our utter dependence on God for His mercy and grace. The Holy Spirit leads us from the error of our sinful ways and shows us the way of love and truth. "You will know the truth, and the truth will set you free" (John 8:32).

The conviction of the Holy Spirit applies the truths of God revealed in the Scriptures to our minds, affections, and wills. We know them to be true when we consider them carefully and prayerfully. When we listen to the Spirit we find true peace, joy, and reconciliation with God—things that are quite different from shame and guilt.

The Power of Humility

Several years ago I went to the Franciscan Renewal Center in Portland, Oregon, to receive spiritual direction and enjoy a much-needed rest. Spiritual direction originated with the Catholic and Episcopalian traditions but has been embraced recently by evangelical Christians who call it a "midwife for the soul." It is a listening ear for God's movement in your life. I so appreciated my experiences with spiritual direction that I went on to receive formal spiritual direction training.

Nestled in the foothills southeast of Portland, the Franciscan Renewal Center is a quiet, majestic facility that exudes peace from the moment you meander down the winding drive. No neon signs announce its presence. The retreat center is available only to those who seek it out—a reminder to me of the gospel message.

During this visit I felt depleted of energy. I was battling warring desires to both slow down and, at the same time, maintain my frenetic schedule. I needed relief, and I wanted it immediately. I had packed my impatience in my suitcase right next to my Bible.

I settled easily into the spartan room, having been there a few times before. Here was the simple bed, the small desk and chair, the outdated lamp, and the sweeping view of the hillside and verdant valley—just as I had left them some years earlier. My tension drained as I turned off my cell phone and packed it away for the next 36 hours. I must admit to a twinge of anxiety (what if someone had to reach me?) but I decided that perhaps my availability wasn't as important as I sometimes imagined it to be.

After ten wonderful hours of sleep, I immediately began looking forward to my hour with Sister Camille. This woman, who had dedicated her life to appreciating the pleasures of God, reserved an hour just for me. I went to her comfortable waiting room and prayed quietly.

Lord, I want some answers today. I want to know exactly what I should do with my work schedule. I want help with balance. I need to hear from You. Please use Sister Camille to speak to me. I am listening. Amen.

As I look at that prayer today, I wonder if God ever loses patience with us. Although I insisted that I was paying attention, Sister Camille would aptly point out that perhaps I was talking more than I was listening.

Sister Camille invited me into her consulting room. She was dressed in a soft, light-colored blouse and pressed slacks. Her silver hair was neatly combed. The room held a pastoral picture of an Italian scene, a small blue vase with fresh flowers on the table, and two comfortable chairs.

"Tell me, David, what is on your mind? What is God doing in your life these days?"

"I am frustrated," I said.

"About what?"

I proceeded to tell her about my impatience with finding balance in my life. I poured out to her that I had prayed about this issue, but as quickly as an answer seemed to come it evaporated.

"I am pressured by opposing desires. I want to slow down, meditate on Scripture, write in my journal, and enjoy friends and family. But at the same time, I want to keep working at the office, seeing my clients, teaching spiritual formation classes, and running a lay counseling program. Regardless of how much energy I expend, I can't fit it all into my life. I'm not sure what to do."

Sister Camille listened for a few more minutes as I continued to complain about my problem. When I finished, she shared her thoughts.

"Perhaps it is time to stop working on the problems and let the problems work on you. You wrestle with them, but you don't sit with them. You don't let them work on you."

Her words hit me like a rock to the side of the head. I looked at her in amazement—how had she come up with something so profound, so simple, so perfectly suited to my needs?

I sat for several moments before thanking her for her insights and returning to my room to journal and pray.

I was struck by her wisdom and how similar it was to the counsel of poet Rainier Maria Rilke to "live the questions" that will one day help us live into the answers.

To live out the counsel given by Rilke and Sister Camille, I would need to live in humility. I would need to admit that I did not have all the answers to my life and would need to wait patiently until those answers would be revealed to me. This is a difficult course of action for someone who desperately wants control over his life.

Another voice advocating humility as an ounce of prevention against issues of guilt and shame comes from the Scriptures. The apostle Paul offers us a fresh perspective on the importance of humility. He warned the Corinthians, "If you think you are standing firm, be careful that you don't fall!" (1 Corinthians 10:12). He had already pointed to humility as a source of power in their lives: "Consider your calling, brethren, that there were not many wise according to the flesh, not many mighty, not many noble; but God has chosen the foolish things of the world to shame the wise, and God has chosen the weak things of the world to shame the things which are strong, and the base things of the world and the despised God has chosen, the things that are not, so that He may nullify the things that are, so that no one should boast before God" (1 Corinthians 1:26-29 NASB).

Paul adds later, in another letter to the church at Corinth:

[God] has said to me, "My grace is sufficient for

you, for power is perfected in weakness." Most gladly, therefore, I will rather boast about my weaknesses, so that the power of Christ may dwell in me. Therefore I am well content with weaknesses, with insults, with distresses, with persecutions, with difficulties, for Christ's sake; for when I am weak, then I am strong (2 Corinthians 12:9-10).

Here we see the nature of God's wisdom. I want to be in control, to conquer all of my weaknesses and character defects. My perfectionist tendencies shout that I must straighten up my act before God can really use me. Of course, God says no to this nonsense. True power comes from Him, and He can use all of my weaknesses as strengths.

God uses us not in spite of our weaknesses but because of them and through them. Paul was not preaching from the abstract when he offered us these powerful truths—he was speaking from personal experience. He was greatly troubled by some malady and prayed for relief, as we often do. He apparently never found full healing for his problem but learned in the process a more important lesson. The tremendous promise of power in weakness was God's answer to Paul's cry for help with his "thorn in the flesh."

My meeting with Sister Camille has transformed my life in a small way. I think about her words often. I have a card pasted to my desk at work saying, "Don't just work on things; let things work on me." I remember that weakness can be a friend. We achieve our greatest successes from a position of humility. That is where we discover wonderful things about ourselves. God is good and redeems our weaknesses.

God's Freedom

Too often, freedom is something we take for granted. Yet once it is threatened, we value it above nearly everything else. My clients who have spent time in prison talk passionately about the importance of being free. Little things they once took for granted—the opportunity for privacy, the ability to shop for themselves, the right to sleep without a stranger lying inches away—they now appreciate.

Although you may never have been incarcerated, you have spent time in your own prison. You have been wracked with nagging guilt without knowing how to pry open the bars. You have been hemmed in on every side with the voices of guilt and shame as your constant companions. You have wanted to scream, "Leave me alone! I want to live my own life!" Now, after incorporating the principles presented in this book, you have access to the keys that will open the prison doors. At last, you can walk free.

Danger is ahead, however. Once handed the keys to the gates, many choose to remain in the world where they have become dependent and comfortable. This is a common phenomenon. Creatures of habit, we often choose our familiar misery rather than the unknown. I encourage you to risk—to choose life and freedom.

Becoming free is not only an external move that includes unshackling handcuffs, shedding sterile orange jail suits, or walking through iron gates. Real freedom also means a freedom of the soul. For this we need God's help. We need His power to break the shackles of our unhealthy thoughts and behaviors. God is ready and willing to provide for us—to help us make this choice for freedom. In this spirit, I encourage you to memorize and meditate upon a favorite Scripture of mine.

> The Spirit of the Lord is on me, because he has anointed me to preach good news to the poor. He has sent me to proclaim freedom for the prisoners and recovery of sight for the blind, to release the oppressed, to proclaim the year of the Lord's favor (Luke 4:18).

Prevention, Not Perfection

Even if you are empowered with skills from the Relationship Doctor, you should not expect the path to be perfectly smooth.

Practicing steps of prevention does not automatically produce perfection. Expect to encounter struggles along the way.

Henri Nouwen, in his book *The Wounded Healer*, admits that even as a trained healer, he endured struggles. He had to learn, as do you and I, that we will always be on a path of healing. One never reaches flawlessness. And perhaps that is a good thing. On our path to healing, we maintain some level of vulnerability—in part because we always need to rely on the Lord's strength. Nouwen says that we are best able to minister to others when we have been wounded. Here again we hear echoes of the apostle Paul's words that tell us God's strength shines through our weakness.

Because we are human, we are not perfect. Relapses happen to the best of us. Symptoms have a way of reappearing and reminding us that we still have work to do. This is not necessarily a bad thing, especially if we have learned to make friends with our symptoms and heed the subtle urgings of the Holy Spirit. As long as we are alive, we will experience some degree of distress resulting from guilt and shame.

Our focus should be on prevention and progress—not perfection. I find comfort in this thought. I can take active steps to live a spiritually and emotionally healthy life, but I am not required to have an answer to every problem.

I continue to seek balance in my life between work and play. I have not perfected how to live out all the relationship advice I dispense so easily. I am a work in progress—and therefore an even more compassionate healer.

You too are a work in progress, and your healing story can be helpful to others. Don't wait until you are fully healed to begin sharing the good news with those around you. The world can't wait!

A Full Dose

It is time to leave the doctor's office and head back to your daily life. If you have worked hard to identify your symptoms and determine an accurate diagnosis, you are ready to select the appropriate remedy.

In this final section of *The Relationship Doctor's Prescription for Living Beyond Guilt*, we have talked about maintaining a lifestyle that will keep you as free as possible from guilt and shame in the future. Now that we have walked together through this book, you are aware of how debilitating guilt and shame can be. Perhaps you have struggled with real guilt resulting from mistakes you have made that require forgiveness, false guilt distributed by people who would have you live a life other than your own, or shame that has grown out of abuse in your past. Perhaps your issue has been the result of conviction of the Holy Spirit calling you to a holier life. Whatever your situation, I hope above all that you are listening to yourself and to God and have made decisions to change and grow.

Think of this book as a prescription pad, offering medicine for the days ahead. Don't take only enough medicine to alleviate the symptoms temporarily. Only a full-strength dose will lead to a long-term cure.

Refer back to this book often as a guide on your journey to emotional and spiritual health. Now, as you move forward, I pray that you will live a life free from guilt and shame as you embrace the liberty that Christ offers to you.

God bless.

Notes

Chapter 1—Listen to Your Pain

1. Scott Peck, *The Road Less Traveled* (New York: Simon and Schuster), 15.

2. Mark Nepo, *The Book of Awakening* (Berkeley: Conari Press, 2000), 358.

3. Lynn Larkin, "Say Goodbye to Guilt," *Evergreen Monthly*, September 1999.

Chapter 3—Conviction Helps—Shame Doesn't

1. Robert McGee, *The Search for Significance* (Nashville: Thomas Nelson, 1998), 131-132.

2. John Bradshaw, *Creating Love* (New York: Bantam, 1992), 32.

3. Anne Lamott, *Traveling Mercies* (New York: Pantheon Books, 1999), 135.

Chapter 4—Why Do I Feel Guilty Before I've Done Anything Wrong?

1. Steve Chandler, *17 Lies That Are Holding You Back* (Los Angeles: Renaissance Books, 2000), 41.

2. Kevin Leman, *Measuring Up* (Old Tappan, NJ: Fleming H. Revell, 1988), 122.

3. Charles Whitfield, *Boundaries and Relationships* (Deerfield Beach, FL: Health Communications, Inc., 1993), 144.

4. Patricia Evans, *The Verbally Abusive Relationship* (Avon, MA: Adams Media Corporation, 1996), 50-51.

5. John Bradshaw, *Creating Love* (New York: Bantam, 1992), 69.

6. Matthew McKay, *Self-Esteem* (New York: MJF Books/Fine Communications, 1997), 10.

7. Harriet Goldhor Lerner, *The Dance of Anger* (New York: Harper and Row, 1985), 3, 15.

Chapter 5—Truth and Consequences

1. Gail Sheehy, *New Passages* (New York: Ballantine Books, 1995), 237.

2. Mark Goulston, *The 6 Secrets of a Lasting Relationship* (New York: The Berkeley Publishing Group, 2001), 148.

3. Jordan Paul and Margaret Paul, *Do I Have to Give Up Me to Be Loved by You?* (New York: MJF Books, 1983), 212.

Chapter 7—Defeating the Invisible Giant

1. Kevin Leman, *Measuring Up* (Old Tappan, NJ: Fleming H. Revell, 1988), 132-139.

2. John Bradshaw, *Healing the Shame That Binds You* (Deerfield Beach, FL: Health Communications, 1988), 10.

3. Ibid., 115.

Chapter 8—A Light at the End of the Tunnel

1. Donald Miller, *Blue Like Jazz* (Nashville: Thomas Nelson, 2003), 138.

2. Hannah Whitall Smith, *A Christian's Secret to a Happy Life*. Available online at www.ccel.org.

3. Richard Mayhue, *A Christian's Survival Guide* (Nashville: Thomas Nelson, 1996), 166-167.

Dr. Hawkins is interested in
hearing about your journey and may be
contacted through his website at
www.YourRelationshipDoctor.com

Other Great Harvest House Books
by David Hawkins

When Pleasing Others Is Hurting You

When you begin to forfeit your own God-given calling and identity in an unhealthy desire to please others, you move from servanthood to codependency. This helpful guide can get you back on track.

Saying It So He'll Listen

Dr. Hawkins offers straightforward, intelligent counsel for dealing with sensitive topics in a relationship. You will find new motivation to press through to the goal of effective communication: reconciliation and greater intimacy in marriage.

Nine Critical Mistakes Most Couples Make

Dr. Hawkins shows that complex relational problems usually spring from nine destructive habits couples fall into, and he offers practical suggestions for changing the way husbands and wives relate to each other.

When Trying to Change Him Is Hurting You

Dr. Hawkins offers practical suggestions for women who want to improve the quality of their relationships by helping the men in their lives become healthier and more fun to live with.

When the Man in Your Life Can't Commit

With empathy and insight Dr. Hawkins uncovers the telltale signs of commitment failure, why the problem exists, and how you can respond to create a life with the commitment-phobic man you love.

The Relationship Doctor's Prescription for Healing a Hurting Relationship

Dr. Hawkins uncovers the hidden reasons why you may be hurting emotionally. He offers practical steps you can take to heal your hurt and suggests a plan for preventing needless pain in the future.

The Relationship Doctor's Prescription for Living Beyond Guilt

Dr. Hawkins explains the difference between real guilt, false guilt, shame, and conviction, bringing these feelings into the light and demonstrating how they can reveal the true causes of emotional pain.